Franc

ois Bernier, Henry Oldenburg

The History of the Late Revolution of the Empire of the Great Mogul

Vol. 1-2. Second Edition

Franc

ois Bernier, Henry Oldenburg

The History of the Late Revolution of the Empire of the Great Mogul
Vol. 1-2. Second Edition

ISBN/EAN: 9783337320904

Printed in Europe, USA, Canada, Australia, Japan

Cover: Foto ©ninafisch / pixelio.de

More available books at **www.hansebooks.com**

THE
HISTORY
OF
The Late Revolution
OF THE
EMPIRE
OF THE
GREAT MOGOL:

Together with the moſt conſiderable Paſſages for 5 years following in that Empire.

To which is added,

A LETTER to the Lord *COLBERT*, touching the Extent of *Indoſtan*; the Circulation of the Gold and Silver of the World, to diſcharge it ſelf there; as alſo the *Riches, Forces,* and *Juſtice* of the ſame: And the Principal Cauſe of the Decay of the States of *Aſia*.

By Monſ^r F. BERNIER, Phyſitian of the Faculty of *Montpelier*.

Engliſh'd out of French.

THE SECOND EDITION.

LONDON Printed, and Sold by *M. Pitt* at the *Angel*, and *S. Miller* at the *Star*, in St. *Paul's Church yard*; and *J. Starkey* at the *Miter* near *Temple-Bar*. 1676.

An EXTRACT of a
LETTER
Written to Mr. H. O.
FROM
Monſieur DE MONCEAUX
THE YOUNGER,
Giving a Character of the BOOK
here Engliſhed, *and its* AUTHOR.

Virtue ſometimes is no leſs intereſſed than Affection: Both, Sir, are glad to receive from time to time pledges mutually anſwering for thoſe that have united themſelves in a cloſe correſpondence. Yours indeed ſhould demand of

An Extract of a Letter

me such, as might be a security to you for the advance you have been pleased to make me of your Friendship. But since at present I have nothing worth presenting you with; and yet am unwilling to give you any leisure to be diffident of my realness, or to repent for having so easily given me a share in your esteem, I here send you a *Relation* of INDOSTAN, in which you will find such considerable Occurrences, as will make you confess, I could not convey to you a more acceptable Present, and that Monsieur *Bernier*, who hath written it, is a very Gallant Man, and of a mould, I wish all Travellers were made of. We ordinarily travel more out of *Unsettledness* than *Curiosity*,

Written to Mr. H. O.

riofity, with a defign to *fee* Towns and Countries rather than to *know* their Inhabitants and Productions; and we ftay not long enough in a place, to inform our felves well of the Government, Policy, Interefts and Manners of its People. Monfieur *Bernier*; after he had benefitted himfelf for the fpace of many years by the converfe of the famous *Gaffendi*, feen him expire in his arms, fucceeded him in his Knowledge, and inherited his Opinions and Difcoveries, embarqued for *Ægypt*, ftay'd above a whole year at *Cairo*, and then took the occafion of fome *Indian* Veffels, that Trade in the Ports of the *Red Sea*, to pafs to *Suratte*; and after Twelve years abode at
the

An Extract of a Letter

the Court of the GREAT MOGOL, is at laſt come to ſeek his reſt in his native Countrey, there to give an Accompt of his Obſervations and Diſcoveries, and to poure out into the boſom of *France*, what he had amaſſed in *India*.

Sir, I ſhall ſay nothing to you of his Adventures, which you will find in the Relations that are to follow hereafter, which he abandons to the greedineſs of the Curious, who prefer their ſatisfaction to his quiet, and do already perſecute him to have the ſequel of this Hiſtory. Neither ſhall I mention to you the hazards he did run, by being in the Neighbourhood of *Mecca*; nor of his prudent Conduct, which made him merit the eſteem

Written to Mr. H. O.

esteem of his Generous *Fazelkan*, who since is become the first Minister of that Great Empire, whom he taught the principal Languages of *Europe*, after he had Translated for him the whole Philosophy of *Gassendi* in *Latin*, and whose leave he could not obtain to go home, 'till he had got for him a select number of our best *European* Books, thereby to supply the loss he should suffer of his Person. This, at least, I can assure you of, *that* never a Traveller went from home more capable to observe, nor hath written with more knowledge, candour, and integrity; *that* I knew him at *Constantinople*, and in some Towns of *Greece*, of so excellent a Conduct, *that* I proposed him to my self for a Pattern in the Design I then had, to carry my Curiosity as far as the place where the Sun riseth; *that* I have often drowned in the sweetness of his entertainment the bitternesses, which else I must have swallowed all alone, in such irksome and unpleasant passages, as are those of *Asia*.

Sir, You will do me a pleasure to let me know the sentiment, your Illustrious SOCIETY hath of this Piece. Their Approbation begets much emulation among the Intelligent, who all have no other Ambition than to please them. I my self must avow to you, that if I thought I could merit so much, I should not so stiffly oppose, as I do, the
Publi-

Written to Mr. H. O.

Publication of the Obfervations and Notes I have made in the *Levant*. I fhould fuffer my Friends to take them out of my Cabinet, where, from the flight value I have for them, they are like to lye imprifoned, except the KING my Mafter, by whofe Order I undertook thofe Voyages, fhould abfolutely command me to fet them at liberty, and to let them take their courfe in the world. Mean time, Sir, you will oblige me, to affure thofe GREAT MEN, who this day compofe the moft knowing Company on Earth, of the Veneration I have for the Oracles that come from their Mouth, and that I prefer their *Lyceum* before that of *Athens*; and laftly, that

An Extract of a Letter, &c.

that of all their Admirers there is none, that hath a greater Concern for their Glory, than

Paris, Julij 16, 1670.   *De* MONCEAUX.

The

The HEADS of the Principal Contents of this HISTORY:
Added by the *English* Interpreter.

1. WHat *depth of Policy and Craft was used by* Aureng-Zebe, *the* Heros *in this History, and the Third of the Four Sons of* Chah-Jehan *the* Great Mogol, *to supplant all his Brothers, and to settle himself in the Throne: And how the first Foundation thereof was laid by the* Vifier *of the King of* Golkonda, *and the sickness of* Chah-Jehan *the Father of* Aureng-Zebe.

2. *A mixture of Love-Intrigues, practised by the Princess* Begum-Saheb, *one of the two Daughters of the* Great Mogol, Chah-Jehan.

3. *How* Aureng-Zebe *having overcome all his Brothers, did secure his Father, and others, whom he had cause to be jealous of.*

4. *How*

The Heads of this History.

4. How the Neighbours of the Empire of Mogol *demeaned themselves towards the new Emperour*, Aureng-Zebe; *and what Embassies were dispatched to him, first by the* Usbec-Tartars *(where a Description of that Countrey and People;) then the* Dutch *of* Suratte; *as also from* Mecca, *from* Arabia Felix, *from* Ethiopia *and* Persia; *together with an Account of their respective Instructions, Receptions, Entertainments and Dismissions; particularly of that of the* Hollanders, *securing and improving their Trade by this their Embassie.*

5. Aureng-Zebe's *singular prudence, and indefatigable pains, in managing the Government himself; and how he treated him that endeavoured to perswade him to take his ease and pleasure, now he was established.*

6. Aureng-Zebe's *distaste against his Favourite-Sister*, Rauchenara-Begum, *occasioned by some Love-Cabals.*

7. *His great Care in appointing a Governour and Tutor to his Third Son* Sultan Ekbar.

8. *With what wisdom and severity*
Aureng-

The Heads of this History.

Aureng-Zebe *received and treated his Pedantick Tutor, who expected to be made a great Lord for his former service; together with a Model for the sutable Education of a Great Prince, prescribed by* Aureng-Zebe *on this occasion.*

9. *In what credit* Judiciary Astrology *is over all* Asia.

10. *How the Kings of* India *make themselves Heirs of all the Estate of those that dye in their service.*

11. *Of the Reciprocal Appearance of Kindnesses between* Aureng-Zebe *and his Imprison'd Father and Sister.*

12. *What pass'd between* Aureng-Zebe *and* Emir-Jemla, *who had laid the first Ground-work to* Aureng-Zebe's *Greatness.*

13. *What in these Revolutions was transacted about the Bay of* Bengale *and the Heathen Kingdom of* Rakan.

14. *How* Aureng-Zebe *carried himself towards his two Eldest Sons,* Sultan Mahmoud *and* Sultan Mahum: *And how, for a Trial of the Obedience and Courage of the latter, he commanded him to kill a certain Lion, that did great mischief*

The Heads of this History.

mischief in the Countrey; together with the success thereof.

15. *Divers Particulars, shewing the Interest between* Indostan *and* Persia, *supposed by this Author to be unknown, or at least not well known hitherto.*

16. *How generously* Aureng-Zebe *recompensed those that had faithfully served him in these Revolutions.*

17. *Some Account of that small Kingdom of* Kachimere, *or* Cassimere, *represented as the Paradice of the* Indies; *concerning which the Author affirms, that he hath a particular History of it in the* Persian *Tongue.*

18. *A considerable Relation of* Suratte's *being strangely surpriz'd and plunder'd, by a stout Rebel of* Visapour; *and how the* English *and* Dutch *saved themselves and their Treasure in this bold Enterprize.*

19. *A particular Account both of the former and present State of the whole Peninsule of* Indostan; *the occasion of its Division into divers Sovereignties, and the several Arts used to maintain themselves one against another; particularly of the present Government and State*

of

The Heads of this History.

of the Kingdoms of Golkonda *and* Visapour, *and their Interests in reference to the* Great Mogol.

20. *Of the Extent of* Indostan, *and the Trade which the* English, Portugueses, *and* Hollanders, *have in that Empire; as also of the vast quantities of* Gold *and* Silver, *circulated through the World, and conveyed into* Indostan, *and there swallowed up, as in an Abyss.*

21. *Of the many Nations, which in that vast Extent of Countrey cannot be well kept in subjection by the* Great Mogol.

22. *Of the* Great Mogol's *Religion, which is* Mahumetan, *of the* Turkish, *not* Persian *Sect.*

23. *Of his* Militia, *both in the Field and about his Person; and how the same is provided for, employed, punctually paid, and carefully distributed in several places.*

24. *Of the* Omrahs, *that is, the* Great Lords *of* Indostan; *their several Qualities, Offices, Attendants.*

25. *The Artillery of the* Mogol, *great and small, very considerable.*

26. *Of his Stables of Horses, Elephants,* Camels, Mules, &c.

27. *Of*

The Heads of this History.

27. *Of his* Seraglio.

28. *Of his vast Revenues and Expences.*

29. *What Prince may be said to be truly Rich.*

30. *An important State-Question Debated,* viz. *Whether it be more expedient for the Prince and People, that the Prince be the sole Proprietor of all the Lands of the Countrey over which he Reigns, yea or no?*

THE

THE
HISTORY
OF
The Late Revolution
OF THE
DOMINIONS
OF THE
GREAT MOGOL.

THE desire of seeing the World having made me Travel into *Paleſtina* and *Egypt*, would not let me ſtop there; it put me upon a reſolution to ſee the *Red Sea* from one end to the other.

other. I went from *Grand Cairo*, after I had staid there above a year; and in two and thirty hours, going the *Caravan*-pace, I arrived at *Suez*, where I embarked in a Galley, which in seventeen days carry'd me, always in fight of land, to the Port of *Gidda*, which is half a days journey from *Mecca*. There I was constrained (contrary to my hopes, and the promise which the *Beig* of the *Red Sea* had made me) to go a shore on that pretended Holy Land of *Mahomet*, where a Christian, that is not a Slave, dares not set his foot. I staid there four and thirty days; and then I embarked in a small Vessel, which in fifteen days carried me along the Coast of *Arabia the Happy* to *Moka*, near the Streight of *Babel-mandel*. I resolved to pass thence to the Isle of *Masowa* and *Arkiko*, to get as far as *Gonder*, the Capital Town of the Country of *Alebech*, or the Kingdom of *Æthiopia*; but I received certain information, that, since the *Portuguese* had been killed there by the intrigue of the Queen Mother, or expelled,

of the Empire of MOGOL. 3
pelled, together with the Jesuit Patriarch, whom they had brought thither from *Goa*, the *Roman* Catholicks were not safe there; a poor Capuchin having lost his head at *Suaken*, for having attempted to enter into that Kingdom: That indeed, by going under the name of a *Greek* or an *Armenian* I did not run so great hazard, and that even the King himself, when he should know, that I could do him service, would give me Land to Till by Slaves, which I might buy if I had money; but that undoubtedly they would forthwith oblige me to Marry, as they had lately done a certain Frier, who had passed there under the name of a *Greek* Physitian; and that they would never suffer me to come away again.

These considerations, among others, induced me to change my resolution. I went aboard of an *Indian* Vessel; I passed those Streights, and in two and twenty days I arrived at *Surratte* in *Indostan*, the Empire of the *Great Mogol*, in the Year 1655. There I found,
B 2 that

that he who then Reigned there, was call'd *Chah-Jehan*, that is to say, King of the World; who, according to the History of that Countrey, was Son of *Jehan-Guyre*, which signifieth Conquerour of the World, Grandchild of *Ekbar*, which is Great, and that thus ascending by *Houmayons*, or the Fortunate, Father of *Ekbar*, and his other Predecessors, he was the *Tenth* of those that were descended from that *Timur-Lengue*, which signifieth the *Lame Prince*, commonly and corruptly call'd *Tamerlan*, so renowned for his Conquests; who Married his near Kinswoman, the only Daughter of the Prince of the Nations of *Great Tartary*, call'd *Mogols*, who have left and communicated their Name to the strangers, that now Govern *Indostan*, the Countrey of the *Indians*; though those that are employ'd in publick Charges and Offices, and even those that are listed in the *Militia*, be not all of the Race of the *Mogols*, but strangers, and Nations gather'd out of all Countries, most of them *Persians*, some *Arabians*, and some *Turks*.

For,

of the Empire of MOGOL.

For, to be esteem'd a *Mogol*, 'tis enough to be a stranger white of Face, and a *Mahumetan*; in distinction as well to the *Indians*, who are brown, and *Pagans*, as to the *Christians* of *Europe*, who are call'd *Franguis*.

I found also at my arrival, that this King of the World, *Chah-Jehan*, of above seventy years of Age, had four Sons and two Daughters; that, some years since, he had made these four Sons Vice-Kings or Governours of four of his most considerable Provinces or Kingdoms; that it was almost a year that he was fallen into a great sickness, whence it was believed he would never recover: Which had occasioned a great division among these four Brothers (all laying claim to the Empire) and had kindled among them a War which lasted about five years, and which I design here to describe, having been present at some of the most considerable Actions, and entertained for the space of eight years at that Court, where Fortune and the small stock of Money (left me after divers encoun-

encounters with Robbers, and the expences of a Voyage of six and forty days from *Suratte* to *Agra* and *Dehli*, the Capital Towns of that Empire) obliged me to take a Salary from the *Grand Mogol* in the quality of a Physitian, and a little while after from *Danech-mend-Kan*, the most knowing Man of *Asia*, who had been *Bakchis* or Great Master of the Horse, and was one of the most powerful and the most considerable *Omrahs* or Lords of that Court.

The *Eldest* of these four Sons of *Chah-Jehan* was call'd *Dara*, that is *Darius*. The *Second* was call'd *Sultan Sujah*, that is the Valiant Prince. The Name of the *Third* was *Aurenge-Zebe*, which signifies the Ornament of the Throne. That of the *Fourth* was *Morad-Bakche*, as if you should say, Desire accomplished. Of the two Daughters, the eldest was call'd *Begum-Saheb*, that is the Mistress Princess; and the youngest *Rauchenara-Begum*, which is as much as Bright Princess, or the Splendour of Princesses.

'Tis

'Tis the Custom of the Countrey, to give such Names to their Princes and Princesses. Thus the Wife of *Chah-Jehan*, so renown'd for her Beauty, and for having a Tomb, which much more deserved to be reckon'd among the Wonders of the World, than those unshapen Masses, and those heaps of stones in *Egypt*, was called *Tage-Mehalle*, that is to say, the Crown of the *Seraglio*; and the Wife of *Jehan-Guyre*, who hath so long Govern'd the State, whilst her Husband minded nothing but Drinking and Divertisements, was first called *Nour-Mehalle*, and afterwards, *Nour-Jehan-Begum*, the Light of the *Seraglio*, the Light of the *World*. The reason, why they give such kind of Names to the Great Ones, and not Names from their Land or Dominion (as is usual in *Europe*) is, because all the Land being the Kings, there are no Marquisates, Earldoms and Dutchies, of which the Grandees might bear their Names; all consists in Pensions either of Land or ready Money, which

which the King giveth, increaseth, retrencheth, and takes away, as seems good unto him: And 'tis even for this reason, that the *Omrahs* have also no other but such Names; one *(for example)* being called *Raz-Audaze-Kan*, *i.e.* a Thunderer; another, *Safe Cheken-Kan*, a Breaker of Ranks; a third, *Bare-Audaze-Kan*, a Man of Lightening; others, *Dianet-Kan*, or *Danechmend-Kan*, or *Fazel-Kan*, *i.e.* the Faithful Lord, the Intelligent, the Perfect, and the like.

Dara, the Eldest Son, wanted not good Qualities. He was Gallant in Conversation, Witty in Reparties, exceeding Civil and Liberal, but entertained too good an opinion of his person, esteeming himself alone capable of all, and thinking it scarce possible that any Body was able to give him counsel; insomuch, that he would give reproachful Names to those who pretended to advise him in any thing; whereby it came to pass, that even those, who were most affectionate to him, were shie to discover to him

of the Empire of MOGOL. 9

him the moft fecret Intrigues of his Brothers. Befides, he was apt to be tranfported with paffion, to menace, to injure, to affront, even the greateft *Omrahs* or Lords; but all paffed over like a flafh of Light. Though he was a Mahumetan, and publickly expreffed in the ordinary Exercifes of Religion to be fo, yet, in private, he was Heathen with the Heathen, and Chriftian with the Chriftians. He had conftantly about him of thofe Heathen Doctors, to whom he gave very confiderable Penfions, and who (as was faid) had inftilled into him Opinions contrary to the Religion of the Land; of which I may touch fomething hereafter, when I fhall come to fpeak of the Religion of the *Indians* or *Gentiles*. He alfo hearkened of late very willingly to the Reverend Father *Buzee* a Jefuit, and began very well to relifh what he fuggefted. Yet there are fome who fay, that at the bottom he was void of all Religion, and that whatever he pretended in it, was only for curiofity, or, as others fay, out of of policy, to make himself beloved by the Christians, who are pretty numerous in his Artillery; but above all, to gain the Affection of the *Rajas* or Soveraign Gentiles, that were Tributary to the Empire, and to make them of his party upon occasion. Mean time, this hath not much furthered his Affairs, on the contrary, it will appear in the sequel of this History, that the pretence used by *Aureng-Zebe*, his third Brother, to Cut off his Head, was, that he was turned *Kafer*, that is to say, an Infidel, of no Religion, an Idolater.

Sultan Sujah, the second Brother, was much of the humour of *Dara*, but he was more close and more settled, and had better Conduct and Dexterity. He was fit to manage an Intrigue well, and he made, under hand, friends by the force of presents, which he heaped upon the great *Omrahs*, and principally upon the most powerful *Rajas*, as *Jessomseigne*, and some others; but he did somewhat too much indulge his pleasures, in entertaining an extraordinary

ordinary number of Women, among whom when he was, he spent whole days and nights in drinking, singing, and dancing. He made them presents of very rich Apparel; and he encreased or lessened their pensions according as the fancy took him: By which kind of Life his Affairs did languish, and the affections of many of his people cooled. He cast himself into the Religion of the *Persians*, although *Chah-Jehan*, his Father, and all his Brothers, were of the *Turkish*. 'Tis known that *Mahumetanism* is divided into several Sects, which made that famous *Check-Sady*, Author of the *Goulistan*, say in Verse, which is to this effect in Prose; *I am a Dervich Drinker, I seem to be without Religion, and I am known of sixty two Sects.* But of all those Sects there are two principal ones, whose Partisans are mortal Enemies to one another. The *one* is that of the *Turks*, whom the *Persians* call *Osmantous*, that is, Sectators of *Osman*; they believing that 'tis he that was the true and lawful Successor of *Mahomet*, the Great Caliph

Caliph or Soveraign Prieſt, to whom alone it did appertain to interpret the *Alcoran*, and to decide the Controverſies to be met with in the Law. The *other* is that of the *Perſians*, whom the *Turks* call *Chias*, *Rafezys*, *Aly-Merdans*, that is, Sectaries, Hereticks, Partiſans of *Aly*, becauſe they believe, contrary to the belief of the *Turks*, that this ſucceſſion and pontifical Authority, which I juſt now intimated, was due only to *Aly* the Son-in-law of *Mahomet*. It was by reaſon of State that *Sultan Sujah* had embraced this latter Sect, conſidering that all the *Perſians* being *Chias*, and moſt of them, or their Children, having the greateſt power at the Court of *Mogol*, and holding the moſt important Places of the Empire, he had moſt reaſon to hope, that, when occaſion ſerved, they would all take his part.

Aureng-Zebe, the third Brother, had not that Gallantry, nor ſurpriſing Preſence of *Dara*, he appeared more ſerious and melancholy, and
was

of the Empire of MOGOL. 13

was indeed much more judicious, understanding the World very well, and knowing whom to chuse for his service and purpose, and where to bestow his favour and bounty most for his interest. He was reserved, crafty, and exceedingly versed in dissembling, insomuch that for a long while he made profession to be *Fakire*, that is, Poor, *Dervich*, or Devout, renouncing the World, and faining not to pretend at all to the Crown, but to desire to pass his Life in Prayer and other Devotions. In the mean time he failed not to make a' party at Court, especially when he was made Vice-King of *Decan*; but he did it with so much dexterity, art, and secrecy, that it could hardly be perceived. He also had the skill to maintain himself in the Affection of *Chah-Jehan* his Father, who although he much loved *Dara*, could yet not forbear to shew that he esteemed *Aureng-Zebe*, and judged him capable to Reign; which caused jealousie enough in *Dara*, who began to find it, insomuch that he could not
hold

hold from saying sometimes to his friends in private; *Of all my Brothers I apprehend only this Nemazi*, that is, this *Bigot*, this great Praying-man.

Morad-Bakche, the Youngest of all, was the least dextrous, and the least judicious. He cared for nothing but mirth and pastime, to drink, hunt, and shoot. Yet he had some good Qualities; for he was very civil and liberal; he gloried in it, that he kept nothing secret; he despised *Cabals*; and he bragg'd openly, that he trusted only in his Arm and Sword: In short, he was very Brave, and if this Bravery had been accompanied with some Conduct, he would have carried the Bell from all his Brothers, and been King of *Indostan*; as will appear in what is to follow.

Concerning the two Daughters, the Eldest, *Begum-Saheb*, was very Beautiful, and a great Wit, passionately beloved of her Father. It was even rumoured, that he loved her to that degree as is hardly to be imagined, and that he alledged for his excuse, that,

of the Empire of MOGOL. 15

that, according to the determination of his *Mullahs* or Doctors of his Law, it was permitted a Man to eat of the Fruit of the Tree he had planted. He had so great a confidence in her, that he had given her charge to watch over his safety, and to have an Eye to all what came to his Table: And she knew perfectly to manage his humour, and even in the most weighty Affairs to bend him as she pleased. She was exceedingly enriched by great pensions, and by costly presents, which she received from all parts, for such Negotiations as she employed her self in about her Father: And she made also great expences, being of a very liberal and generous disposition. She stuck entirely to *Dara*, her Eldest Brother, espoused cordially his part, and declared openly for him; which contributed not a little to make the Affairs of *Dara* prosper, and to keep him in the affection of his Father; for she supported him in all things, and advertised him of all occurrences: Yet that was not so much, because he was

the

the Eldest Son, and she the Eldest Daughter (as the people believed) a because he had promised her, that as soon as he should come to the Crown he would Marry her; which is altogether extraordinary, and almost never practised in *Indostan*.

I shall not scruple to relate here some of the *Amours* of this Princess although shut up in a *Seraglio*, and well kept, like other Women. Neither shall I apprehend, that I may be thought to prepare Matter for a Romancer; for they are not *Amours* like ours, followed by Gallant and *Comical* Adventures, but attended with Events dreadful and *Tragical*.

Now 'tis reported, that this Princess found means to let a young Gallant enter the *Seraglio*, who was of no great Quality, but proper, and of a good Meen. But among such a number of jealous and envious persons, she could not carry on her business so privily, but she was discover'd. *Chah-Jehan*, her Father, was soon advertised of it, and resolved to surprise her,

her, under the pretence of giving her a Visit, as he used to do. The Princess seeing him come unexpected, had no more time than to hide this unfortunate Lover in one of the great Chaudrons made to Bath in; which yet could not be so done, but that *Chah-Jehan* suspected it. Mean time he quarrelled not with his Daughter, but entertained her a pretty while, as he was wont to do; and at length told her, that he found her in a careless and less neat posture; that it was convenient she should wash her self, and bath oftner; commanding presently, with somewhat a stern countenance, that forthwith a Fire should be made under that Chaudron, and he would not part thence, before the Eunuchs had brought him word, that that unhappy Man was dispatched. Some time after she took other measures, she chose for her *Kane-saman*, that is, her Steward, a certain *Persian* called *Nazerkan*, who was a young *Omrah*, the handsomest and most accomplished of the whole Court, a

C   Man

Man of Courage and Ambition, the Darling of all, infomuch that *Chah-Heftkan*, Uncle of *Aureng-Zebe*, propofed to Marry him to the Princefs: But *Chah-Jehan* received that propofition very ill, and befides, when he was informed of fome of the fecret Intrigues that had been formed, he refolved quickly to rid himfelf of *Nazerkan*. He therefore prefented to him, as 'twere to do him honour, a *Betele*, which he could not refufe to chew prefently, after the Cuftom of the Countrey. *Betele* is a little knot made up of very delicate leaves, and fome other things, with a little Chalk of Sea-Cockles; which maketh the Mouth and Lips of a Vermilion colour, and the Breath fweet and pleafing. This young Lord thought of nothing lefs than being poyfoned: He went away from the Company very jocund and content into his *Paleky*; but the Drug was fo ftrong, that before he could come to his Houfe, he was no more alive.

Rauchenara-Begum never paffed for fo hand-

handsome and spiritual as *Begum-Saheb*, but she was not less cheerful, and comely enough, and hated pleasures no more than her Sister. But she addicted her self wholly to *Aureng-Zebe*, and consequently declared her self an Enemy to *Begum-Saheb* and *Dara*. This was the cause, that she had no great Riches, nor any considerable share in the Affairs of the State: Nevertheless as she was in the *Seraglio*, and wanted no Wit and Spies, she could not but discover many important Matters, of which she gave secret advertisement to *Aureng-Zebe*.

Chah-Jehan, some years before the Troubles, finding himself charged with these four Princes, all come to Age, all Married, all pretending to the Crown, Enemies to one another, and each of them making secretly a Party, was perplexed enough, as to what was fittest for him to do, fearing danger to his own Person, and foreseeing what afterwards befell him: For, to shut them up in *Goualeor*, which is a Fortress where the Princes are ordinarily

narily kept close, and which is held impregnable, it being situated upon an inaccessible Rock, and having within it self good water, and provision enough for a Garrison; *that* was not so easie a thing. They were too potent already, each of them having a Princely Train. And again, he could not handsomely remove them far off, without giving them some Government fit for their Birth; wherein he apprehended they would Cantonize themselves, and become little independent Kings; as actually they afterwards did. Nevertheless, fearing lest they should cut one anothers Throat before his Eyes, if he kept them still at Court, he at last concluded to send them away. And so he sent *Sultan Sujah*, his second Son, into the Kingdom of *Bengale*; his third, *Aureng-Zebe*, into *Decan*; and the youngest, *Morad-Bakche*, to *Guzaratte*; giving to *Dara*, the eldest, *Cabal* and *Multan*. The three first went away very well content with their Government; and there they

Acted

of the Empire of MOGOL.

Acted each the Soveraign, and retained all the Revenues of their respective Countries, entertaining great Troops, under the pretence of bridling their Subjects and Neighbours. As to *Dara*, becaufe the eldest, and designed to the Crown, he stirred not from the Court; which that he should not do, seemed also to be the intention of *Chah-Jehan*, who entertained him in the hopes of succeeding him after his Death. He even permitted then, that Orders were issued out by him, and that he might sit in a kind of Throne, beneath his, among the *Omrahs*; so that it seemed, as if there were two Kings together. But as 'tis very difficult for two Soveraigns to agree, *Chah-Jehan*, though *Dara* shew'd him great Observance and Affection, always harbour'd some diffidence, fearing above all things the *Morsel*; and besides, for as much as he knew the parts of *Aureng-Zebe*, and thought him more capable to Reign than any of the rest, he had always (as they say) some particular correspondence with him. This

This it is, what I thought fit to premise concerning these four Princes, and their Father *Chah-Jehan*; because 'tis necessary for the understanding of all that follows. I esteem'd also, that I was not to forget those two Princesses, as having been the most considerable Actors in the Tragedy; the Women in the *Indies* taking very often, as well as at *Constantinople* and in many other places, the best part in the most important Transactions, though Men take seldom notice of it, and trouble their heads of seeking for other Causes.

But to deliver this History with clearness, we must rise somewhat higher, and relate what passed, sometime before the Troubles, between *Aureng-Zebe*, the King of *Golkonda*, and his Visier *Emir-Jemla*; because this will discover to us the Character and Temper of *Aureng-Zebe*, who is to be the *Heros* of this Piece, and the King of the *Indies*. Let us then see, after what manner *Emir-Jemla* proceeded, to lay the first foundation of the Royalty of *Aureng-Zebe*. Du-

of the Empire of MOGOL.

During the time that *Aureng-Zebe* was in *Decan*, the King of *Golkonda* had for his Visier and General of his Armies this *Emir-Jemla*, who was a *Persian* by Nation, and very famous in the *Indies*. He was not a Man of great Extraction, but beaten in Businefs; a person of excellent parts, and a great Captain. He had the Wit of amassing great Treasures, not only by the Administration of the Affairs of this opulent Kingdom, but also by Navigation and Trade, sending ships into very many parts, and causing the Diamond Mines, which he alone had farmed under many borrowed names, to be wrought with extraordinary diligence. So that people discoursed almost of nothing but of the Riches of *Emir-Jemla*, and of the plenty of his Diamonds, which were not reckon'd but by Sacks. He had also the skill to render himself very potent and considerable, entertaining, besides the Armies of the King, very good Troops for his particular, and above all a very good Artillery, with abundance of

Fran-

Franguys or Christians to manage it. In a word, he grew so rich, and so puissant, especially after he had found a way to enter into the Kingdom of *Karnates*, and to pillage all the ancient Churches of the Idols of that Countrey, that the King of *Golkonda* became jealous of it, and prepared himself to unsaddle him; and that the more, because he could not bear what was reported of him, as if he had used too great familiarity with the Queen his Mother, that was yet beauteous. Yet he discover'd nothing of his Design to any, having patience, and waiting 'till *Emir* came to the Court, for he was then in the Kingdom of *Karnates* with his Army. But one day, when more particular News was brought him of what had passed between his Mother and Him, he had not power onongh to dissemble any longer, but was transported by choler to fall to invectives and menaces: Whereof *Emir* was soon made acquainted, having at the Court abundance of his Wives Kindred, and all
his

of the Empire of MOGOL. 25
his nearest Relations and best Friends possessing the principal Offices. The Kings Mother also, who did not hate him, had speedy information of the same. Which obliged *Emir*, without delay, to write to his only Son, *Mahmet Emir-Kan*, who then was about the King, requiring him to do the best he could to withdraw with all speed from the Court, under some pretence of Hunting, or the like, and to come and joyn with him. *Mahmet Emir-Kan* failed not to attempt divers ways; but, the King causing him to be narrowly observed, none of them all would succeed. This very much perplexed *Emir*, and made him take a strange resolution, which cast the King in great danger to lose his Crown and Life; so true 'tis, that *he who knows not to Dissemble, knows not how to Reign.* He writ to *Aureng-Zebe*, who was then in *Daulet-Abad*, the Capital of *Decan*, about fifteen or sixteen days Journey from *Golkonda*, giving him to understand, *that* the King of *Golkonda* did intend to ruin him and his Family,

not-

notwithstanding the signal Services he had done him, as all the World knew; which was an un-exampled Injustice and Ingratitude; *that* this necessitated him to take his refuge to him, and to intreat him, that he would receive him into his protection; *that*, for the rest, if he would follow his advice, and confide in him, he would so dispose Affairs, that he would at once put into his hands both the King and Kingdom of *Golkonda*. This thing he made very easie, using the following Discourse: You need but take four or five thousand Horse, of the best of your Army, and to March with Expedition to *Golkonda*, spreading a rumour by the way, that 'tis an Ambassadour of *Chah-Jehan* that goes in haste, about considerable Matters, to speak with the King at *Bag-nagner*. The *Dabir*, who is he that is first to be addressed unto, to make any thing known unto the King, is allyed to me, and my Creature, and altogether mine; take care of nothing but to March with expedition, and I will so order it, that without making

you

you known, you shall come to the Gates of *Bag-naguer*; and when the King shall come out to receive the Letters, according to custome, you may easily seize on him, and afterwards of all his Family, and do with him what shall seem good to you; in regard that his House of *Bag-naguer*, where he commonly resides, is unwalked and unfortified. He added, *that* he would make this Enterprise upon his own Charges, offering him fifty thousand *Roupies* a day (which is about five and twenty thousand Crowns) during the whole time of the March.

Aureng-Zebe, who looked only for some such occasion, had no mind at all to lose so fair an one. He soon undertook the Expedition, and did so fortunately manage his Enterprise, that he arrived at *Bag-naguer*, without being otherwise known than as an Ambassadour of *Chah-Jehan*. The King of *Golkonda* being advertised of the arrival of this pretended Ambassadour, came forth into a Garden, according to custome, received him with honour,

nour, and having unfortunately put himself into the hands of his Enemy, ten or twelve Slaves, *Gurgis*, were ready to fall upon and to seize his person, as had been projected; but that a certain *Omrah*, touched with tenderness, could not forbear to cry out, though he was of the party, and a Creature of *Emir*, *Doth not your Majesty see that this is* Aureng-Zebe? *Away, or you are taken.* Whereat the King being affrighted, slips away, and gets hastily on horseback, riding with all his might to the Fortress of *Golkonda*, which is but a short League from thence.

Aureng-Zebe seeing he was defeated in his Design, yet was not therefore discomposed; but seized at the same time on the Royal House, taketh all the rich and good things he finds there; yet sending to the King all his Wives (which over all the *Indies* is very religiously observed;) and goeth to Besiege him in his Fortress. But as the Siege, for want of having brought along all Necessaries, held on
long,

long, and lasted above two months, he received Order from *Chah-Jehan* to raise it, and to retire into *Decan* again; so that, although the Fortress was reduced to extremities, for want of Victuals and Ammunition of War, he found himself obliged to abandon his Enterprise. He knew very well, that it was *Dara* and *Begum* that had induced *Chah-Jehan* to send these Orders, from the apprehension they entertained, that he would become too powerful; but in the mean time he never discover'd any resentment of it, saying only, that he ought to obey the Orders of his Father. Yet he withdrew not, without causing underhand payment to be made to him of all the Charges of his Expedition: Besides, he Married his Son *Sultan Mahmoud* to the Eldest Daughter of that King, with a promise, that he would make him his Successor, causing him also to give him for a Dowry the Fortress and the Appurtenances of *Bamguyre*. He also made the King consent, that all the Silver Money, that should be Coined

Coined for the future in that Kingdom, should bear on one side the Arms of *Chah-Jehan*; and that *Emir-Jemla* should withdraw with his whole Family, all his Goods, Troops, and Artillery.

These two Great Men were not long together, but they framed great Designs: On the way they Besieged and took *Bider*, one of the strongest and most important Places of *Visapour*; and thence they went to *Daulet-Abad*, where they contracted so intimate a Friendship together, that *Aureng-Zebe* could not live without seeing *Emir* twice a day, nor *Emir* without seeing *Aureng-Zebe*. Their Union began to cause a new Face in all the Affairs of those Parts, and laid the first foundations of the Royalty of *Aureng-Zebe*.

This Prince having used the Art to make himself to be called to the Court divers times, went with great and rich presents to *Agra* to *Chah-Jehan*, presenting him his Service, and inducing him to make War against the King

King of *Golkonda*, and him of *Viſa-pour*, and againſt the *Portugals*. At firſt he preſented to him that great Diamond, which is eſteem'd matchleſs; giving him to underſtand, that the precious ſtones of *Golkonda* were quite other things, than thoſe Rocks of *Kandahar*; that *there* it was, where the War ought to be made, to get the poſſeſſion thereof, and to go as far as *Cape Comory*. *Chah-Jehan*, whether it were that he was dazled by the Diamonds of *Emir*, or whether he thought it fit, as ſome believe he did, to have an Army in the Field, ſomewhat to reſtrain *Dara*; whom he found active in making himſelf potent, and who with inſolence had ill treated the Viſier *Sadullah-Kan* (whom *Chah-Jehan* paſſionately loved, and conſidered as the greateſt Stateſman that had been in the *Indies*) cauſing him even to be made away with poyſon, as a Man not of his party, but inclined to *Sultan Sujah*; or rather, becauſe he found him too powerful, and in a condition to be the Umpire of the Crown, if

Chah-

Chah-Jehan should decease; or lastly, because being neither *Persian*, nor of *Persian* Extraction, but an *Indian*, there were not wanting envious persons, who spread abroad, that he entertained in divers places numerous Troops of *Patans*, very Gallant Men, and well paid, with a design to make himself King, or his Son; or at least to expel the *Mogols*, and to restore to the Throne the Nation of the *Patans*, of whom he had taken his Wife. However it be, *Chah-Jehan* resolved to send an Army towards *Decan* under the Conduct of *Emir-Jemla*.

Dara, who saw the consequence of this Affair, and that the sending of Troops for those parts, was to give strength to *Aureng-Zebe*, opposed it exceedingly, and did what he could to hinder it. Nevertheless, when he saw that *Chah-Jehan* was resolute for it, he at last thought it best to consent; but with this condition, that *Aureng-Zebe* should keep in *Daulet-Abad*, as Governour only of the Countrey, without medling at all in the War,

of the Empire of MOGOL.

War, or pretending to Govern the Army; that *Emir* should be the absolute General, who for a pledge of his Fidelity was to leave his whole Family at the Court. *Emir* struggled enough within himself, whether he should agree to this last condition, but when *Chah-Jehan* desired him to give that satisfaction to *Dara*, and promised him, that after a little while he would send him back his Wife and Children, he consented, and Marched into *Decan* towards *Aureng-Zebe* with a very Gallant Army, and without any stop entred into *Visapour*, where he Besieged a strong place called *Kaliane*.

The Affairs of *Indostan* were in that condition, as I have been relating, when *Chah-Jehan* fell dangerously sick. I shall not speak here of his sickness, much less relate the particulars of it. I shall only say this, that it was little sutable to a Man of above seventy years of Age, who should rather think on preserving his strength, than to ruin it, as he did. This sickness did soon allarm and trouble all *Indostan*.

Mighty

Mighty Armies were levied in *Dehly* and *Agra*, the Capitals of the Empire. *Sultan Sujah* did the like in *Bengale*; and *Aureng-Zebe* in *Decan*; and *Mord-Bakche* in *Guzaratte*: All four affembled to themfelves their Allies and Friends; all four write, promife, and form divers Intrigues. *Dara* having furprifed fome of their Letters, fhew'd them to *Chah-Jehan*, and made great noife about them; and his Sifter *Begum* failed not to make ufe of this occafion, to animate the King againft them. But *Chah-Jehan* was diffident of *Dara*, and fearing to be poyfoned, gave order, that particular care fhould be had of what was brought to his Table. 'Twas alfo faid, that he wrote to *Aureng-Zebe*; and that *Dara* being advertifed thereof, could not forbear to menace, and to break into very paffionate expreffions. In the mean time the Diftemper of *Chah-Jehan* lingred, and 'twas bruited every where, that he was dead. Whereupon the whole Court was diforder'd, the whole Town allarm'd, the Shops for many days

days shut up; and the four Sons of the King made openly great Preparations, each for himself: And to say truth, it was not without reason, that they all made ready for War; for they all very well knew, that there was no hopes of quarter, that there was no other way, than to vanquish or dye; to be King or undone, and that he that should be Conquerour would rid himself of all the rest, as formerly *Chah-Jehan* had done of his Brothers.

Sultan Sujah, who had heaped up great Treasures in that rich Kingdom of *Bengale*, ruining some of the *Rajas* or petty Kings that are in those parts, and drawing great Sums from others, took the Field first of all with a puissant Army, and in the confidence he had of all the *Persian Omrahs*, for the Sect of whom he had declared himself, he boldly Marched towards *Agra*, giving out openly that *Chah-Jehan* was dead, that *Dara* had poyson'd him, that he would revenge the death of his Father; and in a word, that he would be King. *Dara* desired *Chah-Jehan*

Jehan to write himself to him, and to forbid him to advance further; which he did, assuring him, that his sickness was not at all dangerous, and that he was already much better. But he having Friends at Court, who assured him that the sickness of *Chah-Jehan* was mortal, he dissembled, and ceased not to advance, saying still, that he knew very well *Chah-Jehan* was dead; and if he should be alive, he was desirous to come and kiss his feet, and to receive his Commands.

Aureng-Zebe immediately after, if not at the same time, taketh the Field also in *Decan*, maketh a great noise, and prepareth to March towards *Agra*. The same prohibition was made to him also, as well from *Chah-Jehan*, as from *Dara*, who threaten'd him. But he dissembleth, for the same reason that *Sultan Sujah* had done, and giveth the like answer. Mean time, finding that his Treasure was low, and his Souldiery very inconsiderable, he devised two artifices, which succeeded admirably well; the one, in regard

of

mpire of MOGOL. 37
akche; the other, in re-
r-Jemla. To Morad-Bakche
ith speed a very fair Letter,
that he had always been
intimate Friend; that, as
he laid no claim at all to
that he might remember,
his Life time made profes-
kire, but that Dara was a
pable to Govern a King-
he was a Kafer, an Ido-
hated of all the greatest
at Sultan Sujah was a Ra-
etick, and by consequence
Indostan, and unworthy
vn: So that, in a word,
one but he (Morad-Bakche)
reasonably pretend to the
that the Crown did expect
the whole Court, which
norant of his Valour,
or him; and that for his
if he would promise him,
King, he would give him
quietly in some Corner
his Empire, there to serve
mainder of his days, he
D 3   was

was ready to make a conjunction with him, to assist him with his Counsel and Friends, and to put into his hands his whole Army, to fight *Dara* and *Sultan Sujah*; that in the mean time he sent him an hundred thousand Rupies (which make about fifty thousand Crowns of our Money) and prayed him to accept thereof as a pledge of his friendship; and *that* he would advise him to come with all possible speed to seize on the Castle of *Suratte*, where he knew to be the Treasure of the Land.

Morad-Bakche, who was neither too rich nor too powerful, received with much joy this proposition of *Aureng-Zebe*, and the hundred thousand Rupies sent by him, and shew'd *Aureng-Zebe*'s Letter to every body, thereby to oblige the Flower of that Countrey to take up Arms for him, and the substantial Merchants to lend him the more willingly such Sums of Money as he demanded of them. He began in good earnest to Act the King, made large promises to all, and, in short,

of the Empire of MOGOL.

short, did so well, that he set a good Army on foot; of whom he singled out some three thousand, who, under the Conduct of *Chah-Abas*, one of his Eunuchs, but a Valiant Man, should go to Besiege *Suratte*.

Aureng-Zebe sent his Eldest Son, *Sultan Mahmoud*, (him whom he had Married to the Daughter of the King of *Golkonda*) to *Emir-Jemla*, who was yet employed in the Siege of *Kaliane*, to perswade him to come to him to *Daulet-Abad*, pretending to have matter of the greatest importance to communicate to him. *Emir*, who soon suspected his intentions, excused himself, saying openly that *Chah-Jehan* was not dead, *that* he had fresh News of his being alive, and *that* besides, all his Family being at *Agra* in the hands of *Dara*, he could by no means assist *Aureng-Zebe*, nor declare himself for him. Whereupon *Sultan Mahmoud* return'd to *Daulet-Abad*, without effecting any thing, and very much dissatisfied with *Emir*. But *Aureng-Zebe* lost no courage for all that, but sent

sent the second time to *Emir*, yet not *Sultan Mahmoud*, but *Sultan Mazum* his Second Son, who presented to him his Fathers Letter, and handled him with that dexterity, sweetness, and protestation of friendship, that it was not possible to resist him. *Emir* therefore pressed the Siege of *Kaliane*, forced the Besieged to Surrender upon Composition, took the choice of his Army, and with all diligence went away with *Sultan Mazum*. At his arrival, *Aureng-Zebe* courted him in the highest degree, treating him no otherwise than with the Name of *Baba* and *Babagy*, that is, Father, Lord-Father; and after an hundred embraces, he took him somewhat aside, and told him (according to what I could learn from persons who knew of it) That it was not just, that having his Family at the Court, he should adventure to do any thing in his behalf that might come to be known; but that, after all, there was nothing so difficult but an expedient might be found. Give me leave therefore, *said he*, to

pro-

of the Empire of MOGOL. 41

propose to you a Design, which at first will possibly surprise you; but, since you apprehend the danger of your Wife and Children that are in Hostage, the best way of providing for their security would be, to suffer me to seize on your person, and to put you in prison. It is out of doubt, that all the World will believe it done in earnest: For who would imagin, that such a person as you would be content to let your self be laid in prison? In the interim, I could make use of part of your Army, and of your Artillery, as you shall judge most proper and convenient: You also could furnish me with a Sum of Money, as you have frequently offered it; and besides, methinks I might tempt Fortune further, and we might together take our measures, to see in what manner I had best to demean my self; if you would also permit, that I might cause you to be transported into the Fortress of *Daulet-Abad*, where you should be Master; and that there I might have you kept by my own Son,

Sultan

Sultan Mazum, or *Sultan Mahmoud*; this would yet better palliate the matter, and I see not, what *Dara* could justly say of it, nor how he could reasonably treat your Wife and Children ill.

Emir, whether it were by reason of the Friendship he had sworn to *Aureng-Zebe*, or for the great promises made to him, or the apprehension he had, of seeing near him *Sultan Mazum*, who stood by, very pensive and well armed, and *Sultan Mahmoud*, who looked grim upon him for his coming away at the sollicitation of his Brother, not at that of his, and had at his very entrance lift up his Foot as if he would have hit him; whatever of these considerations might induce him, consented to all what *Aureng-Zebe* desired, and approved of the Expedient to suffer himself to be imprison'd; so that *Aureng-Zebe* being no sooner gone, but the Great Master of the Artillery was seen to approach with some fierceness to *Emir*, and to command him in the Name of *Aureng-Zebe* to follow him, locking him up in a Chamber, and there

there giving him very good words, whilst all the Souldiery, that *Aureng-Zebe* had thereabout, went to their Arms. The report of the detention of *Emir-Jemla* was no sooner spread, but a great tumult arose; and those, whom he had brought along with him, although astonish'd, yet put themselves into a posture of rescuing him, and with their Swords drawn ran to force the Guards, and the Gate of his Prison; which was easie for them to do: For *Aureng-Zebe* had not with him sufficient Troops to make good so bold an Enterprise; the only Name of *Emir-Jemla* made all tremble. But the whole matter being altogether counterfeited, all these Commotions were presently calmed *by* the intimations that were given to the Chief Officers of *Emir*'s Army, and *by* the presence of *Aureng-Zebe*, who there appeared very resolute with his two Sons, and spoke now to one, then to another, and at last *by* promises and presents, liberally bestowed on those that were concerned. So that all the

Troops

Troops of *Emir*, and even most of those of *Chah-Jehan*, seeing things troubled, and being without their General, and believing *Chah-Jehan* to be dead, or, at best, desperately sick; considering also the ample promises made to them of augmenting their Stipend, and of giving them at that very time three months advance, soon lifted themselves under *Aureng-Zebe*; who having seized on all the Equipage of *Emir*, even his very Camels and Tents, took the Field, resolved to March to the Siege of *Suratte*, and to hasten the taking it in; where *Morad-Bakche* was exceedingly embarrassed, because that his best Troops were employed there, and that he found more resistance in that place than he imagined. But *Aureng-Zebe*, after some days March, was informed, that the Governour had surrendred the Place; for which he sent Congratulations to *Morad-Bakche*, acquainting him withall of his Transactions with *Emir-Jemla*, and assuring him, *that* he had Forces and Money enough, and very good

good Intelligence at the Court; *that* nothing was wanting; *that* he was directly going to *Brampour* and *Agra*; *that* he had expected him on the way, and therefore defired him to joyn with him.

'Tis true, that *Morad-Bakche* found not fo much Money in the Fortrefs of *Suratte* as he had imagined, whether it were that really there was not fo much as was reported, or whether the Governour had diverted a part of it, as fome believed: Yet notwithftanding that little he found there was ufeful to him, to pay the Souldiers that had lifted themfelves in hopes of the advantages, they fhould make of the imagined vaft Treafure of *Suratte*. 'Tis not lefs true, that he had no greater reafon to boaft of the taking of this Place, in regard there was not any Regular Fortification about it; and yet his Army had lain before it above a month, and would never have reduced it without the *Hollanders*, who furnifh'd them with the Invention of Springing a Mine, which

which ruining a great side of the Wall, cast the Besieged into such a consternation, that it made them immediately surrender. The reduction of this Town did much advance his Design, Fame proclaiming immediately throughout these Countries, that *Morad-Bakche* had taken *Suratte*; that he had sprung a Mine, which sounded very big among the *Indians*, who as yet do little understand that practice; and that *there* he had found a vast Treasure. Notwithstanding this great noise, and all the first advantages, joyned to all those frequent Letters and great Promises of *Aureng-Zebe*, the Eunuch *Chah-Abas*, a Man of good Sense, of a great Heart, and exceedingly affectionate to the Service of his Master, was not of opinion, that *Morad-Bakche* should so much tye himself in interest to *Aureng-Zebe*, or precipitate his conjunction with him, but advised, that he should amuse him with words, and let him advance alone towards *Agra*; that in the mean time there would come certain News

of

of the sickness of *Chah-Jehan*; that he should first see, what Channel Affairs would run in; that he should Fortifie *Suratte*, as a very good Post, able to render him Master of a very large and rich Countrey; and that perhaps in time he might seize *Brampour*, which is a very considerable Passage of a River, and as 'twere a Bar of *Decan*. But the continual Letters and Protestations of *Aureng-Zebe*, joyned to the small Forces, Artillery, and Treasure of *Morad-Bakche*, blinded with an excessive ambition to Reign, made him regardless of all other considerations; so that he went away from *Amadevad*, abandon'd *Guzaratte*, and took his way through the Woods and Mountains, with all expedition, to be at the Rendevouz, where *Aureng-Zebe* had looked for him these two or three days.

Great Solemnities of Joy were made at the conjunction of the two Armies, the Princes visited one another, *Aureng-Zebe* made a hundred protestations and no less promises to *Morad-Backche*,

Bakche, assured him afresh, and solemnly, of his not caring for the Crown, as also of his being there for no other end than to assist him against *Dara*, their Common Enemy, and to place him in the Throne, which expected him.

Upon this Enterview, and confirmation of Friendship, both Armies Marched together, *Aureng-Zebe* continuing always, during the March, in the protestations of Friendship, and in his Courtship to *Morad-Bakche*, treating him never otherwise, whether in publick or private, but with the Title of *Hazaret*, that is, King and Majesty: So that *Morad-Bakche* was fully perswaded, that *Aureng-Zebe* meant sincerely, from an excess of affection towards him; whence he even willingly, and without ceremony, suffer'd the submissions and respects he shew'd him; instead of remembring what had lately passed at *Golkonda*, and of considering, that he, who had thus hazarded himself with so much boldness to usurp a Kingdon, was

not

of the Empire of MOGOL. 49

not of a temper to live and dye a *Fakire.*

These two Armies thus jóyned made a Body considerable enough; which begot a great noise at Court, and gave cause of thoughtfulness, not only to *Dara,* but to *Chah-Jehan* himself, who knew the great parts and subtle Conduct of *Aureng-Zebe*, and the Courage of *Morad-Bakche*; and who foresaw very well, that a Fire was a kindling, which would be very hard to quench. It was to no purpose to write Letters upon Letters, signifying that he was well, and giving Order that they should turn back to their respective Governments, and expressing also, that he would forget all that had passed hitherto. All his *Letters* were not able to hinder their advance; and as the sickness of *Chah-Jehan* did still pass for mortal, there being no persons wanting to bring and spread such News, they still continued to dissemble, giving out, that they were *Letters* counterfeited by *Dara*; that *Chah-Jehan* was dead indeed; but that, in

E case

case he were alive, they would go to kiss his Feet, and deliver him from the hands of *Dara*.

What then should *Chah-Jehan*, this unfortunate King, do, who seeth, that his Sons have no regard to his Orders; who is informed at all hours, that they march apace towards *Agra* in the head of their Armies, and who in this conjuncture finds himself sick to boot in the hands of *Dara*, that is, of a man who breatheth nothing but War; who prepareth for it with all imaginable earnestness, and with all the marks of an enraged resentment against his Brothers? But what could he do in this extremity? He is constrained to abandon to them his Treasures, and to leave them to their disposal. He is forced to send for his old and most trusty Captains, whom he knows for the most part to be not very affectionate to *Dara*; he must command them to fight for *Dara*, against his own Blood, his own Children, and those, for whom he hath more esteem than for *Dara*; he is obliged

of the Empire of MOGOL.

liged forthwith to send an Army against *Sultan Sujah*, because 'tis he that is most advanced; and he is to send another against *Aureng-Zebe* and *Morad-Bakche*, who no less are marching towards him.

Soliman Chekouh, the eldest Son of *Dara*, a young Prince of about Five and twenty years of Age, very proper of Body, and of good Parts and Conduct, generous, liberal, and universally beloved, especially of *Chah-Jehan*, who had already enriched him, and who considered *him* rather for his Successour than *Dara*, was he, that was made General of this Army against *Sujah*. Nevertheless *Chah-Jehan*, who wished much rather, that *Sujah* were return'd to *Bengale*, than that the matter should be tryed by a bloody Combat, which could not be but very Tragical, and wherein he run the hazard of losing one or other of his Sons, gave him for Companion an Ancient *Raja*, called *Jesseigne*, who is at present one of the powerfullest and richest *Rajas* of all *Indostan*, and one

E 2 of

of the ableft in the whole Kingdom, with a fecret Order not to fight, except it were altogether unavoidable; as alfo to endeavour by all means to induce *Sujah* to retire, and to referve his Forces for a better occafion; that is to fay, after they fhould have feen the event of the ficknefs of *Chah-Jehan*, and the fuccefs of *Aureng-Zebe*, and of *Morad-Bache*. But this young Prince, *Soliman Chekouh*, full of heat and courage, breathing after nothing but to fignalize himfelf by fome great action, and *Sultan Sujah* fearing left *Aureng-Zebe* gaining a Battel fhould firft make himfelf Mafter of the Capital Towns of the Empire, *Agra* and *Dehly*; it was impoffible for the *Raja Jeffeigne* to keep them from a Combat. The two Armies are no fooner in fight of one another, but they prepare to fall on, and they were not long from giving fome Vollies of Cannon. I fhall not relate the particulars of this Fight, for, befides that the narration of it would be too long and tedious, in the fequel of this Hiftory we fhall be obliged

liged to describe more considerable ones, by which the Reader will be able to judge of this. 'Tis sufficient to know in general, that the first onset was very sharp and obstinate on both sides, but that at length *Soliman Chekouh* did urge *Sujah* with that force and vigour, that he disorder'd him, and made him fly: So that if *Jesseigne*, and the *Patan Delil-kan*, who was one of the first Captains and a valiant Man, but an intimate Friend of the *Raja*, and did not act but being moved by him, had seconded him in good earnest, 'tis thought that the whole Army of *Sujah* would have been defeated, and himself in danger of being taken: But that was not the Design of the *Raja* to destroy him, no more than it was that of *Chah-Jehan*, who had given him order to the contrary. Thus then had *Sujah* time to retreat, and that without losing any considerable number of his Men; yet because *Soliman Chekouh* kept the field, and brought away some pieces of Artillery, it was presently bruited at Court, that *Sujah* had been totally overthrown. This Defeat purchased great reputation to *Soliman Chekouh*, lessen'd much the esteem of *Sultan Sujah*, and cooled exceedingly all the *Persians* that had an inclination for him.

After that some days were spent in the pursuit of *Sujah*, the Prince *Soliman Chekouh*, who every day received News from the Court, and who learned, that *Aureng-Zebe* and *Morad-Bakche* did approach with great resolution, well knowing, that his Father *Dara* had no great stock of prudence, but good store of secret Enemies, resolved to quit the pursuit of *Sultan Sujah*, and with all speed to return to *Agra*, where in all appearance *Dara* was to give Battel against *Aureng-Zebe* and *Morad-Bakche*. This was the best counsel he could take, for no man doubts, that if he could have been there in good time, *Aureng-Zebe* would not have had the advantage; and 'tis even believed, he would never have hazarded the Combat, the party being too unequal; but the bad fortune of *Dara* did not permit it. Whilst

Whilst all that was thus transacted toward *Elabas*, which is the place where the *Gemna* is joyned to *Ganges*; the Scene was very different on the side of *Agra*. At the Court they were much surprised to hear, that *Aureng-Zebe* had passed the River of *Brampour*, and all the other passages that were most difficult between the Mountains; so that with all haste they sent away some Troops to dispute with him the passage of the River *Eugenes*, whilst the whole Army was making ready. For which purpose, there were chosen two of the most considerable and the most powerful of the Kingdom to command it; the one was *Kasem-Kan*, a renowned Captain and very affectionate to *Chah-Jehan*, but one that had no great inclination to *Dara*, and who went not but to oblige *Chah-Jehan*, whom he saw in the hands of *Dara*: The other was *Jessomseigne*, a potent *Raja*, not inferiour to *Jesseigne*, and Son-in-law to that *Raja Rana*, who was at the time of *Ekbar* so puissant, as if he had been the Emperour of the *Raja's*. *Dara* at their farewel expressed to them great kindness, and presented them nobly; but *Chah-Jehan* took his time, before their departure, to charge them in secret, as he had done the *Raja Jesseigne*, when he went away in the Expedition against *Sultan Sujah* with *Soliman Chekouh*. Neither were they wanting, in their March, to send several times to *Aureng-Zebe* and *Morad-Bakche*, to perswade them to turn back: But this was in vain; their Envoys came not again, and the Army advanced with that diligence, that they saw it much sooner than they thought upon a rising ground, not far remote from the River.

It being then Summer, and the season of the greatest heats, the River was fordable; which was the cause, that at the same time *Kasem-Kan* and the *Raja* prepared themselves to give Battel; besides that, they soon knew the resolution of *Aureng-Zebe*, that he would force them, since that, although his Army was not all come up, he gave them some Vollies of Cannon;

non; his defign being to amufe them, fearing left they themfelves fhould pafs the River, not only to prevent his paffage, but alfo to hinder his Army from repofing, and from taking an advantageous poft; which was indeed in great diforder, and fo tired by their March, and fo faint by the heat, that if at the very firft it had been affaulted, and kept from paffing the Water, it would doubtlefs have been routed without much refiftance. [I was not by in this firft Encounter, but thus it was generally difcourfed of, and it agreeth with the after-relation of many of our *French-men*, who ferved *Aureng-Zebe* in the Artillery.] But they were content to ftay at the River-fide, to keep *Aureng-Zebe* from paffing it, according to the Order they had received.

After that *Aureng-Zebe* had let his Army reft two or three days, and by amufing the Enemy, had fitted it to pafs the River, he made his whole Artillery play, which was very well placed; and he commanded, that under

the

the favour of the Cannon they should pass the River. *Kasem-Kan* and the *Raja*, on their part, discharged theirs also, and did what they could to repulse the Enemy, and to keep him from passing. The Combat was sharp enough at first, and very obstinately maintained by the extraordinary Valour of *Jessomseigne*. For as to *Kasem-Kan*, although a great Captain, and a stout Man, he gave no great proof of his Valour in this occasion; yea, some accuse him of Treachery, charging him that he had in the night caused the Bullets and Powder to be hid under the Sand, there being no more of them to be found after two or three discharges. However it be, the Combat for all that was, as I said, very resolutely carried on, and the passage long disputed. There were Rocks in the Bed of the River, which did much embarass, and the Banks in many places were very high and difficult to climb up. But at last, *Morad-Bakche* cast himself into the water with so much resolution and force, and

shew'd

shew'd so much valour and boldness, that there was no resisting of him. He passed over, and with him a good part of the Army, which made *Kasem-Kan* to give back, and cast *Jessomseigne* into great danger of his person. For by and by he found the whole Body of the Enemy upon him, and without the extraordinary resolution of his *Ragipous*, who almost all were killed about him, he had been a dead man. One may judge of the great danger he was in upon this occasion, by this, that after he had disengaged himself as well as he could, and was come back to his own, not daring to return to *Agra*, because of the great loss he had suffered, of seven or eight thousand *Ragipous* he had but five or six hundred of them remaining.

These *Ragipous*, who take their name from the *Rajas*, that is to say, the Children of the *Rajas*, are from Father to Son such Men as make the Sword their Profession. The *Rajas*, whose Subjects they are, do assign them Lands for their subsistence, on condition to be be always ready to go to War when fummoned. So that one might fay, that they were a fort of Pagan Nobles, if the *Rajas* gave them their Lands in propriety for them and their Children. They are great takers of *Opium*; and I have fometimes wondred at the quantity I have feen them take: They accuftom themfelves to it from their youth. On the day of Battel they double the Dofe, this Drug animating, or rather inebriating them, and making them infenfible of danger; infomuch that they caft themfelves into the Combat like fo many furious Beafts, not knowing what it is to run away, but dying at the feet of their *Raja*, when he ftands to it. They want nothing but Order, Refolution they have enough. 'Tis a pleafure thus to fee them, with the fume of *Opium* in their head, to embrace one another, when the Battel is to begin, and to give their mutual Farewels, as Men refolved to dye. And that they do for this reafon; that the *Great Mogol*, though a *Mahumetan*, and by confequence sequence an Enemy of the Heathen, yet for all that entertains always a good number of *Rajas* in his service, whom he considers as his other *Omrahs,* and imploys in his Armies as if they were *Mahumetans.*

I cannot forbear to relate here the fierce reception, which the Daughter of the *Rana* gave to her Husband *Jessomseigne*, after his defeat and flight. When she heard that he was nigh, and had understood what had passed in the Battel; that he had fought with all possible courage, that he had but four or five hundred Men left; and that at last, not being able to resist any longer the Enemy, he had been obliged to retreat: She, in stead of sending one to receive him, and to console him in his misfortunes, commanded in a dry mood to shut the Gates of the Castle, and not to let this infamous Man enter; that he was not her Husband; that she would never see him; that the Son-in-law of the Great *Rana*, could not have so low a Soul; that he was to remember, that

that being grafted into so Illustrious an House, he was to imitate the Virtue of it; and, in a word, that he was either to vanquish or to dye. A moment after she was of another humour; she commands a Pile of Wood to be laid, that she might burn her self, that they abus'd her; that her Husband must needs be dead; that it could not be otherwise. And a little while after this, she was seen to change her countenance, to fall into passion, and to break out into a thousand reproaches against him. In short, she remained thus transported eight or nine days, without being able to resolve to see her Husband, 'till at last her Mother coming in, brought her in some degree to her self, and comforted her, assuring her, that as soon as the *Raja* had but a little refresh'd himself, he would raise another Army, to fight *Aureng-Zebe*, and repair his Honour at any rate.

By which story one may see a pattern of the Courage of the Women in that Countrey: To which I could add

of the Empire of MOGOL. 63

add something I have seen some of them do, who burned themselves alive after the death of their Husbands; but we must reserve this Discourse for another place, where I shall also shew, that there is nothing which opinion, prepossession, custom, hope, and the point of honour, &c. may not make Men do or suffer.

Dara having understood what had passed at *Eugenes*, fell into that choler against *Kasem-Kan*, that it was thought he would have cut off his Head, if he had been upon the place. He was also transported against *Emir-Jemla*, as the Person that was the first and principal Cause of the Misfortune, and who had furnish'd *Aureng-Zebe* with Men, Money, and Cannon. He is ready to kill his Son *Mahmet Emir-Kan*, and will send his Wife and Daughter to *Basar*, or the Market-place of prostituted Women; and 'tis past doubt, that he would have done some such thing, if *Chah-Jehan*, with much art and prudence, had not moderated the excess of his passion, in

remon-

remonstrating to him, that *Emir-Jemla* had not so little conduct, nor so great a Friendship for *Aureng-Zebe*, as to hazard, and in a manner to sacrifice his Family, for the advancing of his Interest; that *Aureng-Zebe* must needs have gulled and ensnared him, by his usual artifice and cunning.

As for *Aureng-Zebe* and *Morad-Bakche*, the happy success of this first Encounter did so swell their hearts, and gave such Courage to their whole Army, that henceforth they believed themselves invincible, and capable to compass any thing. Besides, *Aureng-Zebe*, the more to animate his Souldiers, bragged openly, that he had Thirty thousand *Mogols* at his devotion in the Army of *Dara*; and there was something in it, as appeared by the sequel. *Morad-Bakche* was for nothing but fighting, and would march with all diligence. But *Aureng-Zebe* represented to him, that it was necessary the Army should refresh themselves for some time upon the Banks of this sweet River; that in the mean time he he would write to all his Friends, and get a full and certain information of the state of the Court, and of the condition of all Affairs. So that he marched not towards *Agra*, 'till he had rested some days, and after that he marched but slowly, to inform himself of all, and to take his time and measures.

Concerning *Chah-Jehan*, when he plainly saw the resolution of *Aureng-Zebe* and *Morad-Bakche*, and that there was no hope left to make them turn back, he was in such a perplexity; that he knew not what to resolve; and foreseeing some great calamity, he would fain have hindred the last decisive Battel, for which he saw *Dara* preparing himself with great eagerness. But what could he do to oppose it? He was yet too weak of his sickness, and saw himself still in the hands of *Dara*, whom, as I have said, he trusted not much: So that he found himself obliged to acquiesce in his Will, and to commit to him all the Forces of the Empire; and to com-

command all Captains to obey him. Immediately all was in Arms: I know not, whether there was ever a more gallant Army seen in *Indostan*. 'Tis said, that there were little less than an hundred thousand Horse, and twenty thousand Foot, with four thousand peeces of Cannon, without reckoning the incredible number of Servants, Followers, Victuallers, whom Historians me thinks do often put into the number of the Combatants, when they speak of those formidable Armies of three or four hundred thousand Men, of which their Books are full. Though this Army was very brave, and strong enough to cut in pieces two or three of such as *Aureng-Zebe* had, in which there were no more than thirty five or forty thousand Men in all, and these tired and harassed by a very long and irksom March, during the height of the Heats; and but a small number of Cannon, in respect of that of *Dara*. Mean time (which seems hard to believe) there was scarce any Body that presaged well for *Dara*, all knowing

of the Empire of MOGOL.

that moſt of the chief *Omrahs* had no affection for him, and that all the good Souldiers that were for him, and whom he might confide in, were in the Army of *Soliman Chekouh*, his Son. And 'twas for this reaſon, that the moſt prudent and the moſt faithful of his Friends, and *Chah-Jehan* himſelf, counſelled him, not to hazard a Battel: *Chah-Jehan* offering, as infirm as he was, that he would go into the Field himſelf, and be carried before *Aureng-Zebe*, to interpoſe; which was looked upon as a very good Expedient for Peace, and for accomodating the Affairs of *Chah-Jehan*. For 'tis certain, that *Aureng-Zebe* and *Morad-Bakche*, would never have had the boldneſs to fight againſt their own Father; and if they ſhould have attempted it, they would have ſmarted for it, becauſe, beſides that the match was not equal, and all the great *Omrahs* were ſo affectionate to *Chah-Jehan*, that they would not have failed to fight reſolutely, if they had ſeen him in the head of the Army; beſides this,

F 2 I ſay,

I say, the Captains themselves o[f]
Aureng-Zebe and *Morad-Bakche*, bor[e]
great affection and respect to th[is]
Prince, whose Creatures they mo[st]
were; and the whole Army, in [a]
manner, was his. So that in all ap[-]
pearance, not one of them woul[d]
have presumed to draw his Sword a[-]
gainst him, nor he been at the pains o[f]
drawing his.

Then they advised *Dara*, that
he would not hearken to this Expe[-]
dient, he should at least not precip[i-]
tate the business, but delay, 'till *Sol[i-]
man Chekouh*, who made all haste t[o]
joyn, were come in. Which w[as]
also very good counsel, in regar[d]
that that Prince was beloved of all[,]
and was lately come home victoriou[s,]
and had the most faithful and the br[a-]
vest Souldiers with him. But *Da[ra]*
would never hearken to any prop[o-]
sition that could be made to him, an[d]
he thought on nothing else but to giv[e]
Battel presently, and to go again[st]
Aureng-Zebe in person. And possibl[y]
he did not amiss, as to his own H[onour,]
not[...]

of the Empire of MOGOL. 69

nour and particular Interest, if he could have commanded Fortune, and made things succeed as he contrived them. For the Considerations he had (as he could not forbear now and then to discover) were some such as these:

He looked upon himself as Master of the Person of *Chah-Jehan*; that he could dispose of him as he pleased; that he was also Possessor of all the Treasures and Forces of the Empire; that *Sultan Sujah* was half ruined; that his two other Brothers, with a weak and tired Army, were come to cast themselves into his hands; that, if he gained the Battel, they could not escape him; that he should all at once be absolute Master, and at the end of all his troubles, and at the height of his wishes, so as no body could conradict him in any thing, or dispute the Crown with him. Whereas if *Chah-Jehan* should take the Field, all Affairs would be accommodated, his Brothers would return to their Governments, *Chah-Jehan*, who began to recover his health, would resume the

the Government as before, and a
things would return into their fir
channel: That, if he should stay fo
Soliman Chekouh, his Son, *Chah-Jeha*
might take some Design to his disa(
vantage, or contrive something wit
Aureng-Zebe; that whatever he cou:
do for gaining the Victory, the Repr
tation, which *Soliman Chekouh* had pu
chased, would still give him all tl
honour of it. And after that, wh
would not he be capable to undertak.
swelled with so much glory and su
cess, and especially being supportec
as he was, by the favour and affectic
of *Chah-Jehan*, and of the greate
part of the *Omrahs*? What did I
know, whether he would keep ar
modesty, or any respect for him, ar
whether his Ambition might not car
him?

These Considerations made *Da*
resolve to stand out against the couni
of all, and to pursue his point. A
for that purpose, he commanded ir
mediately the whole Army to take t
Field, and thereupon came to ta
lea

leave of *Chah-Jehan*, who was in the Fortress of *Agra*. This good old Man was ready to melt in tears, when he embraced him; but withall failed not to represent to him, with a very grave countenance: Well, *Dara*, since thou art resolved to follow thine own will, go, God bless thee, but remember well these few words; *If thou losest the Battel, take heed of ever coming into my Presence.* But this made no great impression upon him; he goeth forth briskly, taketh horse, and seizeth on the Passage of the River *Tchembel*, which is about Twenty Miles from *Agra*; where he fortified himself, expecting his Enemy. But the subtile and crafty *Fakire*, who wanted no good Spies, and people that gave him intelligence of all, and who knew that the Passage was there very difficult, took good heed to attempt the forcing it. He came to encamp himself near it, so that from the Camp of *Dara* one might discover his Tents. But what doth he in the mean time? He inveagles a certain Rebel of *Raja*, called

called *Chempet*, presents him richly, and promiseth him a thousand fine things, if he would let him pass thorough his Territories, that so he might go with speed to gain a certain place, where he knew that the River might be passed on foot with ease. *Chempet* agreeth, and offers of his own accord, that he would himself attend him, and shew him the way through the Woods and Hills of his Countrey. *Aureng-Zebe* raised his Camp the same night, without any noise, leaving some of his Tents to amuse *Dara*, and marching night and day, made such haste, that he was almost as soon on the other side of the River, as *Dara* could have notice of it. Which obliged *Dara* to abandon the River there, and to leave all his Fortifications, and to follow his Enemy, who, he was told, did advance with great diligence towards *Agra*, to gain the River of *Gemna*, and there without trouble, and at his ease, to enjoy the water, to fortifie, and to fix himself well, and so to expect *Dara*. The place where

where he encamped is but five leagues from *Agra*, it was formerly called *Samonguer*, and now *Fateabad*, which is to say, *Place of Victory*. A little while after, *Dara* also came to encamp there, nigh the Bank of the same River, between *Agra* and the Army of *Aureng-Zebe*,

The two Armies were there between three and four days in sight of one another, without fighting. Mean time *Chah-Jehan* wrote several Letters to *Dara*, that *Soliman Chekouh* was not far off; that he should not precipitate; that he should come near *Agra*, and chuse an advantageous place to fortifie himself 'till he came. But *Dara* answer'd, that before three days were passed, he would bring to him *Aureng-Zebe* and *Morad-Bakche* tyed hand and foot, to do with them what he should think fit. And without expecting any longer, he began at that very hour to put his Army in Battel array.

He placed in the Front all his Cannon, causing them to be tyed the one to the other with Chains, to shut the

the paffage to the Cava
thefe Peeces of Cannon,
front-wife a great number
mels, on the forepart o
whereof they faften a fm
the bignefs of a double
Man fitting on the hin(
Camel, being able to cl:
charge without lightin
thefe Camels ftood the
of the Mufqueteers. Of
the Army, which chiefly
Cavalry, furnifh'd with
Arrows, (as ordinarily ai
that is, at prefent, whit
humetans, ftrangers, as *Pe*
Arabians, and *Usbecks*;
Sword, and a kind of H
commonly are the *Ragi*
thefe, I fay, there were
different Bodies. The 1
was committed to *Calil-ulla*
Thirty Thoufand *Mogol*
Command; for he was
Bakchis, that is, Great M
Cavalry, in the place of .
Kan, that was afterwards

who voluntarily refigned this Office, feeing that he was not well beloved of *Dara*, for having always highly maintained againſt him the Intereſt and Authority of *Chah-Jahan.* The left Wing was given to *Ruſtam-Kan Dakny*, a very renowned and very valiant Captain, together with the *Raja Chatrefale*, and the *Raja Ramfeigne Routlé*.

On the other fide, *Aureng-Zebe* and *Morad-Bakche* put alſo their Army almoſt into the fame Order; except that in the midſt of the Troops of fome *Omrahs*, they had hid fome fmall Field-Peeces, which was, as was faid, after the way and Art of *Emir-Jemla*, and with no ill effect.

They hardly made uſe of any more Art, than what hath been now related; only they placed here and there fome Men cafting *Bannes*, which is a kind of Granado faſtened to a ſtick, that may be caſt very far through the Cavalry, and which extremely terrifieth Horſes, and even hurts and kills fometimes.

All

All this Cavalry turns about very easily, and they draw their Arrows with marvellous swiftness; one Man being able to draw six of them, before a Musqueteer can twice discharge his Musquet. The same Cavalry keeps also very close in several Troops under their respective Officers, especially when they are going to fight hand to hand. But after all, I see not, that this way of putting an Army in array, is any great matter, in comparison of our Armies, when in good order.

All things being thus disposed, the Artillery began to play on both sides; for 'tis always the Cannon that makes the prelude amongst *them*; and the Arrows were now seen to fly through the Air, when unexpectedly there happen'd to fall a Storm of Rain, so violent, that it interrupted the Combat. The Rain ceasing, the Cannon began afresh to roar; and then it was that *Dara* appeared, who being mounted upon a proud Elephant of *Ceilau*, commanded that an Onset should be made on all sides; and himself advanced

into

of the Empire of MOGOL. 77

into the midst of the Body of the Cavalry, directly towards the Enemies Artillery, who received him warmly, kill'd store of Men about him, and put into disorder, not only the Main Body which he commanded, but also the other Bodies of the Cavalry that followed him. Yet notwithstanding, because he was seen to keep firm upon his Elephant, without any appearance of giving back, and was observed to look every where about him with an undaunted look, and to make signs with his hands to advance and to follow him, this disorder soon ceased, every one resuming his Rank, and advancing in the same pace with *Dara*. But he could not reach the Enemy, without receiving another Volley of Cannon-shot, which caused a second and great disorder in his Men, and made a good part of them recoyl; yet he,. without any change in his countenance, stood to it, encouraging his Troops, and gave still signs, that they should follow him, and advance with speed without any

loss

loss of time. Thus pressing vigorously forward, he forced the Enemies Artillery, broke the Chains, entred into their Camp, and made a Rout in their Camels and Infantry, and in every thing he met with on that side; opening also a good passage to the Cavalry that followed him. Then it was, that the Enemies Cavalry facing him, a sore Combat began. A showre of Arrows fill'd the Air from both sides, *Dara* himself putting his hand to that work :. But, to say truth, these Arrows do but little execution; more of them are lost in the Air, or broken on the ground, than hit. The first Discharges of Arrows being made, they fought hand to hand with their Sables, *pesle mesle*, and the Combat was stoutly maintain'd on both sides. *Dara* is still seen to continue firm on his Elephant, encouraging, making a noise, and giving signs on all sides; and at last advancing with so much resolution and force, against all that opposed him ·in his March, that he overthrew the Cavalry, and made them to retire and run away. *An-*

of the Empire of MOGOL.

Aureng-Zebe, who was not far from thence, and mounted also on an Elephant, seeing this great disorder, was in great trouble, and laboured with all his might to remedy it; but to no purpose. He made the Main Body of his best Cavalry advance, to try whether he could make head against *Dara*; but it was not long before this Body also was forced to give back, and to retreat in great disorder, whatever *Aureng-Zebe* could say or do to hinder it. Mean time let us take notice of his courage and resolution: He saw that almost the whole Body of his Army was disordered, and in a flying posture, in so much that he had not a thousand Men about him that kept their standing; (some told me, that there were scarce five hundred:) He saw, that *Dara*, notwithstanding the difficulty of the way, which was uneven, and full of holes in divers places, made as if he would rush in upon him: Yet, for all this, he lost no courage, and was so far from being struck with fear, or from retreating, that

that he stood firmly to it, and call
by name most of his Captains th[at]
were about him, crying out to the[m]
Delirane Kodahé, (these are his ov[n]
words,) that is, *Courage my old Frien[d],
God is*: What hope is there in flyin[g]
Know you not, where is our *Deca[n]*.
Kodahé, *Kodahé*, *God is*, *God is*. A[nd]
that none might doubt of his bei[ng]
undaunted, and that he thought [of]
nothing less than running away;
commanded before them all (oh stran[ge]
extremity!) that forthwith Chai[ns]
should be fastened to the feet of [his]
Elephant; and was going to fast[en]
them in good earnest, but that th[ey]
all declared their courage and resol[u]
tion, to live and dye with him.

Dara in the interim endeavoured [to]
advance upon *Aureng-Zebe*, though [he]
was yet at a good distance from hin[,]
and though the difficulty of the w[ay]
embarassed and retarded him muc[h,]
he meeting also with some resistanc[e]
even from those disordered Horse [of]
the Enemy, that cover'd all high a[nd]
low places where he was to Marc[h,]
A[nd]

of the Empire of MOGOL. 81

And this Encounter with *Aureng-Zebe* was looked upon as *the* thing, that was to assure *Dara* of the Victory, and to decide the Battel. And doubtless, he would have overcome all these difficulties, and *Aureng-Zebe*, with the small number left him, would not have been able to bid head to this victorious Army, if *Dara* had known how to profit of the prise he had in his hands. But here he failed; of which I shall now shew the occasion, and how thereby the Scale was turned to *Aureng-Zebe*'s advantage.

Dara perceived that his left Wing was in great disorder, and he was informed, that *Rustam-Kan* and *Chatre-sale* were killed; that *Ramseigne Routle* had too far advanced, that he had indeed forced the Enemy, and made way through the midst of them; but that now he was surrounded every way, and in very great danger. This it was, which made *Dara* desist from his design of making directly towards *Aureng-Zebe*, that he might go to succour his left Wing. There at first

G the

the Battel was also very sharp, but *Dara* at last carried it, forcing and routing all, yet so, as that there still remained something that resisted and stopped him. Mean time, *Ramseigne Routlé* fought with so much courage and vigour as was possible. He wounded *Morad-Bakche*, and came so near him, that he began to cut the Girdles of his Elephant, to make him fall down; but the valour and good fortune of *Morad-Bakche* gave not time enough for it. In short, never any Man fought and defended himself more bravely, than *Morad-Bakche* did on this occasion: All wounded as he was, and pressed by the *Ragipous* of *Ramseigne Routlé*, who were round about him, he was not daunted, nor gave way in the least, but knew so well to take his time, that, although he was, besides defending himself, to cover with his Shield a Son of his, but of seven or eight years of Age, who was sitting on his side, he made an Arrow-shot so luckily at *Ramseigne Routlé*, that it made him fall dead to the ground.

Dara

of the Empire of MOGOL.

Dara soon heard the sad News of this Accident; but at the same time he understood also, that *Morad-Bakche* was in very great danger; the *Ragipous* fighting furiously, and like Lions, to revenge the death of their Master. And though he saw, on that side the way was very difficult, and that he still found some small Body opposing and retarding him; yet he was determined to rush through to *Morad-Bakche*: And doubtless this was the best he could do, and that, which was capable to repair the fault he had committed in not doing his business thoroughly with *Aureng-Zebe*. But his bad fortune kept him from it, or rather; one of the blackest Treacheries that ever was imagined, and the greatest oversight that was ever committed, did cause the entire loss and ruin of *Dara*.

Calil-ullah-Kan (he that commanded the Thirty Thousand *Mogols*, which made the right Wing, and were alone able to defeat the whole Army of *Aureng-Zebe*) did; whilst *Dara* and his

his left Wing fought with so much courage and success, keep off, as idle as if he were not concerned in the fray, not permitting any one of his Horsemen to shoot an Arrow, with a pretence, that they were for a Reserve, and that he had express order not to fight but in the last extremity. But the true cause was, that he reserved in his breast the rancour of an old Affront, done him by *Dara*, when he commanded him to be struck. But after all, this Treachery would have done no great mischief, if this infamous Man had contented himself with this first Effect of his Resentment: Behold, how far he carried his rage, and revengefulness! He cut himself off from his Main Body, and taking only a few Men with him, rid with all possible speed towards *Dara*, at the same time when he was turning to fall on *Morad-Bakche*, and being come so near as to make himself be heard, cryed out with all his force; *Mohbareck-bad, Hazaret, Salamet, Elhamdul-ellah*; God save your Majesty, you have

of the Empire of MOGOL.

have obtained the Victory; what will you do any longer upon your Elephant? Is it not enough, that you have expoſed your ſelf ſo long? If the leaſt of thoſe ſhots, that have been made into your *Daïs,* had reached your Perſon, what would have become of us? Are there Traitors wanting in this Army? In the Name of God come down quickly and take Horſe. What remains more to be done, than to purſue thoſe Run-aways. Let us do ſo, nor let us ſuffer, that they ſhould eſcape our hands!

If *Dara* had had wit enough to diſcover the cheat, and to conſider upon a ſudden the conſequences of his not appearing any more upon the Elephant, and being no more ſeen by the whole Army, always eying him, or rather, if he had preſently commanded to cut off the Head of this Paraſitical Traitor, he had been Maſter of all. But the good Prince ſuffered himſelf to be blinded by theſe ſweet words: He hearkened to this advice, as if it had been very true and very ſincere;

sincere; he descended from his Elephant, and took Horse. But I know not, whether there passed one quarter of an hour, but he perceived the Treachery of *Calil-ullah-Kan*, and repented himself extremely of the great fault he had committed. He looks about him, he seeketh, he asketh where he is; he saith, he is a Traitor, he will kill him. But the perfidious Villain is by this time at a good distance; the occasion is lost. Would it be believed, that as soon as the Army perceived *Dara* to be no more upon the Elephant, they imagined that there was Treason, that *Dara* was killed; and all were struck with such a terrour, that every one thought on nothing, but how to escape the hands of *Aureng-Zebe*, and to save himself? What shall I say? All the Army disbands and flyeth. A sudden and strange revolution! He that saw himself just now victorious, finds himself in a few moments vanquished, abandoned, and obliged to fly himself to save his life. *Aureng-Zebe*, by holding out firm a

quarter

of the Empire of MOGOL. 87

quarter of an hour upon his Elephant, feeth the Crown of *Indostan* upon his Head; and *Dara*, for having come down a little too soon, feeth himself precipitated from the Throne, and the most unfortunate Prince of the World. Thus Fortune taketh pleasure, to make the gain or loss of a Battel, and the decision of a great Empire, depend upon a nothing.

These great and prodigious Armies, 'tis true, do sometimes great things; but when once terrour seizeth, and disorder comes among them, what means of stopping the Commotion? 'Tis like a great River broke through its Dams; it must over-run all, without a Remedy. Whence it is, that as often as I consider the condition of such Armies, destitute of good order, and marching like flocks of sheep, I perswade my self, that, if in these parts one might see an Army of five and twenty thousand Men, of those old Troops of *Flandres*, under the conduct of *Monsieur le Prince*, or of *Monsieur de Turenne*, I doubt not at all,

but

but they would trample under foot a.
those Armies, how numerous soeve[r]
they were. And this it is, that now
maketh me not find it any longe[r]
strange or incredible, what we ar[e]
told of ten thousand *Greeks*; and o[f]
fifty thousand Men of *Alexander*, over-
coming six or seven hundred thousan[d]
Men of *Darius*; (if it be true, tha[t]
there were so many, and that the Hi-
storian did not reckon the Servants,
and all those Numbers of Men, which
were to follow the Army, to furnish i[t]
with Forage, Cattel, Corn, and all
other necessaries.) Bear only the first
brunt, which would be no very difficult thing for us to do; and behold,
they are all astonish'd: Or, do like
Alexander, set vigorously upon one
place, if that hold not out, (which will
be very hard of them to do) you may
be sure the work is done; all the rest
presently take fright and flight together.

Aureng-Zebe, encouraged by such a
wonderful success, is not wanting to
turn every stone, to employ skill,
dex-

of the Empire of MOGOL. 89
dexterity, subtilty, craft, courage, to profit by all the advantages, which so favourable an occasion puts into his hands. *Calil-ullah-Kan* is presently with him, offering him his service, and all the Troops he could be Master of. He, on his side, wants not words of thanks and acknowledgments, nor a thousand fair promises: But he was very cautious to receive him in his own name; he carried him presently and presented him to *Morad-Bakche*, who, as we may easily think, received him with open arms; *Aureng-Zebe* in the mean time congratulating and praising *Morad-Bakche*, for having fought so valiantly, and ascribing to him all the honour of the Victory; treating him with the Title of King and Majesty before *Calil-ullah-Kan*, giving him uncommon respect, and doing submissions to him becoming a Subject and Servant. In the interim, he labours night and day for himself, he writeth round about to all the *Omrahs*, making sure to day of one, and next day of another. *Chah-hest-Kan*,

his

his Uncle, the great and old Enem[y]
of *Dara*, by reason of an Affront [he]
had received from him, did the sam[e]
for him on his part; and as he is t[he]
Person who writeth best and subtille[st]
of the Empire of *Indostan*, so he con[-]
tributed not a little by his Cabals [to]
the advancement of the Affairs [of]
Aureng-Zebe, making strong Parti[es]
every where against *Dara*.

In the mean time let us still observ[e]
the artifice and dissimulation of *A[u]-
reng-Zebe*: Nothing of what he dot[h]
treateth, promiseth, is for himself[,]
or in his own Name; he hath sti[ll]
(forsooth) the design of living as [a]
Fakire: All is for *Morad-Bakche*, 'tis h[e]
that commands; *Aureng-Zebe* doth no[-]
thing; 'tis *Morad-Bakche* that doth al[l;]
'tis he that is designed to be King.

As for the unhappy *Dara*, he come[s]
with all speed to *Agra*, in a desperat[e]
condition, and not daring to go se[e]
Chah-Jehan, remembring, doubtless[,]
those severe words which he let fall
when he took leave of him before th[e]
Battel, *viz*. That he should remembe[r]
no[t]

before him, if he were
Yet, for all that, the good
ent secretly a trusty Eu-
, to comfort him, to af-
the continuance of his
declare to him his trouble
tune, and to remonstrate
the Case was not yet de-
idering that there was a
with *Soliman Chekouh*, his
should go to *Dehli*, where
d a thousand Horse in the
; and *that* the Governour
els had order to furnish
oney and Elephants; for
t he should not go further
ls must; *that* he would
o him: And lastly, *that*
knew how to find out and
g-Zebe.
en informed, that *Dara*
uch a confusion, and sunk
t he had not the power
ord to the Eunuch, nor
to send any one to *Chah*
that, after having sent
to *Begum-Saheb*, his Sister,
he

he went away at mid-night, tak[ing]
with him his Wife, his Daught[er]
and his Grand-child *Sepe-Chekouh*;
that (which is almoſt incredible)
was attended with not above three
four hundred perſons. Let us le[ave]
him in his Voyage to *Dehli*, and [stay]
at *Agra*, to conſider the dexterity [and]
craft, wherewith *Aureng-Zebe* proc[ee]
ded to manage Affairs.

He well knew, that *Dara*, and th[ose]
of his Party, could yet place ſo[me]
hopes in the victorious Army of *S[epe-]
man Chekouh*, and therefore he reſol[ved]
to take it from him, or to make
uſeleſs to him. To this end, he wr[ote]
Letters upon Letters to the *Raja* [Jef-]
ſeigne, and to *Delil-Kan*, who w[ere]
the chief Heads of the Army of *S[epe-]
man Chekouh*, telling them, that th[ere]
was no hope left for *Dara* and [his]
Party; that he had loſt the Batt[le,]
that his whole Army had ſubmit[ted]
to him; that all had abandon'd hi[m,]
that he was fled alone towards *Del[hi,]*
that he could never eſcape him, a[nd]
that Orders were diſtributed ev[ery]
wh[ere]

of the Empire of MOGOL. 93
here to seize on him. And as for
hah-Jehan, that he was in a condi-
on hopeless of recovery; that they
ould take good care of what they
id to do; and if they were Men of
iderstanding, and would follow his
rtune, and be his Friends, they
ould seize on *Soliman Chekouh*, and
ing him to him.
Jesseigne found himself perplex'd e-
)ugh, what he should do, still much
)prehending *Chah-Jehan* and *Dara*,
id more, to lay hands upon a Royal
erson, well knowing, that some mis-
lief might therefore fall on him,
oner or later, even from *Aureng-Zebe*
mself. Besides, he knew that *Soli-*
an Chekouh had too much courage to
: himself be taken after that manner,
id that he would rather dye in de-
iding himself. Behold therefore,
hat he at last resolved! After having
ken counsel with *Delil-Kan*, his great
iend, and after they had renew'd to
e another the Oath of mutual Fi-
lity, he went directly to the Tent
Soliman Chekouh, who with great
im-

impatience expected him, (for he a
had heard the News of the Defeat
Dara his Father) and had already
vers times sent for him. To him
frankly discover'd all things, shew
him the Letter of *Aureng-Zebe*, tc
him what course was best for him
take, represented to him the dang
he was in; that there was no real(
he should trust in *Delil-Kan*, or in *Daou
Kan*, or in the rest of his Army; b
that, as soon as he could, he shou
gain the Mountains of *Serenague*
that that was the best Expedient
could take; that the *Raja* of that Cou
trey being in unaccessible places, ai
not apprehending *Aureng-Zebe*, wou
doubtless receive him gladly; and, f
the rest, he would soon see how thin;
would go, and be always in a conc
tion to come down from the Mou
tains, when he should think good.

The young Prince understood we
enough by this kind of discourse, th
there was no ground to trust henc
forth in this *Raja*, and that there w:
no more safety for his Person; an
th

at the rather, becaufe he knew that *lil-Kan* was altogether devoted to m, and he faw well enough, that ere was a neceffity to take this courfe ɡefted. Whereupon he foon comanded, that his Baggage fhould be it up to march towards the Mounins. Some of his moft affectionate iends, as a good number of *Manfebɪrs*, of *Sajeds*, and others, put themves in order to attend him; the reft the Army, altogether aftonifh'd, main'd with the *Raja*. But that, hich was very mean for a great *Raja*, d a very fordid barbaroufnefs, was, at he and *Delil-Kan* fent under hand me to fall upon his Baggage, who o took other things, and among em an Elephant laden with Rupies Gold, which caufed a great difder among thofe fmall Troops that low'd him; and which was an ocion, that many of them return'd d abandon'd him; and invited alfo e Countrey-people to fet upon his en, pillaging them, and even kilg fome of them: Yet he made a
shift

shift to gain the Mountains, with his Wife and Children, where the *Raja* of *Serenaguer* received him with all the honour and civilities he could defire, assuring him, that he was in safety, as much as if he were King of that Countrey, and that he would protect and assist him with all his Forces. In the mean time, behold what happened on *Agra's* side.

Three or four days after the Battel of *Samonguer*, the Victorious *Aureng-Zebe*, together with *Morad-Bakche*, came directly to the Gate of the Town into a Garden, which may be a little League distant from the Fortress, and sent from thence an able Eunuch, and one of those whom he most confided in, to *Chah-Jehan*, to salute him with a thousand fair protestations of his affection and submission; that he was exceedingly sorry for what had passed, and for having been obliged, by reason of the ambition and evil designs of *Dara*, to proceed to all those extremities; that, for the rest, he rejoyced extremely to hear, that he began to find

of the Empire of MOGOL. 97
find himself better, and that he was come thither for no other end than to receive his Commands. *Chah-jehan* was not wanting to exprefs to the Eunuch much satisfaction, as to the proceedings of *Aureng-Zebe*, and to receive the submiffions of this Son with all poffible appearances of joy; though he saw very well, that matters had been carried too far, and sufficiently knew the reserved and crafty humour of *Aureng-Zebe*, and his secret paffion for Reigning; and that therefore he was not much to be trusted, for all his fair words. And yet notwithstanding he suffers himself to be circumvented, and in stead of playing the surest Chart, *by* using his utmost power, *by* stirring, *by* appearing, *by* causing himself to be carried through the Town, and *by* affembling all his *Omrahs*, (for it was yet time to do all this) he goes about to out-wit *Aureng-Zebe*, him that was his Crafts-Master, and attempts to draw him into a snare, wherein he will be found taken himself. He then sends also an Eunuch

H to

to this Son, to let him know, that he well underſtood the ill conduct, and even the incapacity of *Dara;* that he could not but call to mind the particular inclination he always had and expreſſed towards him, that he could not doubt of his affection; and laſtly, that he ſhould come to ſee him, and to adviſe with him what was fit to be done in theſe diſorders; and that he paſſionately wiſhed to embrace him.

Aureng-Zebe, on his ſide, ſaw alſo well enough, that he was not to truſt too much to the words of *Chah-Jehan,* knowing eſpecially, that *Begum-Saheb,* his Enemy as well as Siſter, was night and day about him, and that 'twas very probable, he acted nothing but by her motion. And he apprehended, that if he ſhould come into the Fortreſs, he might be ſeized on, and ill treated; as it was ſaid, that the reſolution was indeed taken to do ſo, and ſeveral of thoſe luſty *Tartarian* Women, which ſerve in the *Seraglio,* were armed to ſet upon him as ſoon as he ſhould enter. Whatever it be, he would

of the Empire of MOGOL.

would never hazard himself, and yet spread a rumour abroad, that the next day he would go to see his Father *Chah-Jehan*. But when the day was come, he put it off 'till another, and so he delayed it from day to day, without ever making the Visit. In the mean time he continued his secret Negotiations and Cabals, and sounded the mind of all the greatest *Omrahs*, so far, that at last, after he had well and closely laid his Design, and politickly disposed all things for the success thereof, all were amazed to see, that one day, when he had sent *Sultan Mahmoud*, his eldest Son, to the Fortress, under a pretence of seeing *Chah-Jehan* in his name; this young Prince, bold and undertaking, falls presently upon the Guards that were at the Gate, and vigorously driveth all before him, whilst a great number of Men appointed, who were there all ready, did enter with fury, and made themselves Masters of the Walls.

If ever a Man was astonish'd, *Chah-Jehan* was, seeing that he was fallen into the snare which he had prepared for others, that himself was imprison'd and *Aureng-Zebe* Master of the Fortress. 'Tis said, that he presently sent to sound the mind of *Sultan Mahmoud*, promising him upon his Crown and upon the *Alcoran*, that if he would be faithful to him, and serve him in this conjuncture, he would make him King; that he should come presently to see him within, and not lose this occasion: Besides, that it would be an action that would accumulate on him the blessings of Heaven, and an immortal Glory; in regard it would be said forever, that *Sultan Mahmoud* had deliver'd *Chah-Jehan* his Grandfather out of Prison.

And certainly, if *Sultan Mahmoud* had been resolute enough to give this stroke, and *Chah-Jehan* could have come abroad to shew himself to the Town, and to take the Field, no man doubts, but all his great *Omrahs* would have followed him; nor would *Aureng-Zebe* himself have had the boldness nor the savageness to fight against his own

own Father in perſon, eſpecially ſince he muſt have apprehended, that all the world would have abandon'd him, and poſſibly *Morad-Bakche* himſelf. And 'tis indeed the great fault which *Chah-Jehan* is obſerved to have committed after the Battel, and the flight of *Dara*, not to have come out of the Fortreſs. But yet I have converſed with many, who maintained, that *Chah-Jehan* did prudently in it. For this hath been a queſtion much agitated among the Politicians, and there are no Reaſons wanting to countenance the Sentiment of the latter ſort; who alſo add, that Men almoſt always judge of things by the Event; that often very fooliſh Enterpriſes have been obſerved to ſucceed, and which therefore are approv'd by all; that if *Chah-Jehan* had proſper'd in his Deſign, he would have been eſteem'd the moſt prudent and the moſt able Man in the World; but now being taken, he was nothing but a good old Man, that ſuffer'd himſelf to be led by a Woman, his Daughter *Begum*, which

which was blinded by her paffion, and had the vanity to believe, that *Aureng-Zebe* would come to fee her, that the Bird of it felf would fly into the Cage, or at leaft, that he would never be fo bold as to attempt the feizure of the Fortrefs, nor have the power to do fo. Thefe fame Reafoners maintaining alfo ftifly, that the greateft fault that *Sultan Mahmoud* could poffibly commit, was, that he knew not how to take the occafion to affure himfelf of the Crown, by the rareft and the moft generous Action that ever was, to put his Grandfather at liberty, and thus to do himfelf Right and Juftice, as the Soveraign Umpire of Affairs; whereas, as things now ftand, he muft one day go and dye in *Goualeor*. But *Sultan Mahmoud* (whether it was that he fear'd his Grandfather would not keep his word with him, or that he fhould be himfelf detain'd within, or that he durft not play tricks with his Father *Aureng-Zebe*) would never hearken to any thing, nor enter into the Apartment

of

of *Chah-Jehan*, anſwering very cloſely, that he had no order from his Father to go and ſee him, but that he was by him commanded not to return, without bringing him the Keys of all the Gates of the Fortreſs, that ſo he might come with all ſafety to kiſs the Feet of his Majeſty. There paſſed almoſt two whole days before he could reſolve to ſurrender the Keys; during which time, *Sultan Mahmoud* ſtaid there, unalterable in his reſolutions, keeping himſelf upon his Guard night and day, with all his Troops about him; 'till at length *Chah-Jehan*, ſeeing that all his People that were upon the Guard at the little Gate, little by little disbanded, and that there was no more ſafety on his ſide, gave him the Keys, with an order to tell *Aureng-Zebe*, that he ſhould come preſently if he were wiſe, and that he had moſt important things to diſcourſe with him about. But *Aureng-Zebe* was too cunning to commit ſo groſs a fault: On the contrary, he made his Eunuch *Etbarkan* Governour of the Fortreſs, who presently shut up *Chah-jehan*, together with *Begum-Saheb*, and all his Women; causing divers Gates to be walled up, that so he might not be able to write or speak to any body, nor go forth out of his Apartment without permission.

Aureng-Zebe in the mean time writ to him a little Note, which he shew'd to every body before he sealed it; in which, among other things, he told him with dry expressions, that he knew from good hands, that notwithstanding those great protestations of esteem and affection he made to him, and of contempt he made of *Dara*, he had, for all that, sent to *Dara* two Elephants charged with Rupies of Gold, to raise him again, and to recommence the War; and that therefore, in truth, it was not he that imprisoned him, but *Dara*, and that he might thank him for it, as the cause of all these misfortunes; and if it had not been for him, he would have come the very first day to him, and paid him all the most dutiful respects he could

could have looked for from a good Son: That, for the reſt, he begged his pardon, and a little patience; as ſoon as he ſhould have diſenabled *Dara* from executing his evil Deſigns, he would come himſelf and open the Gates to him.

I have heard it ſaid concerning this Note, that *Chah-Jehan* in very deed, the ſame night that *Dara* departed, had ſent to him theſe Elephants laden with Rupies of Gold, and that it was *Rauchenara-Begum* that found a way to diſcover it to *Aureng-Zebe*; as ſhe alſo had detected to him that Plot which was laid againſt him with thoſe *Tartarian* Women; and that *Aureng-Zebe* himſelf had intercepted ſome Letters of *Chah-Jehan* to *Dara*.

I have converſed with others, that maintain there is no ſuch thing, and that this Writing, which *Aureng-Zebe* ſhew'd to all, was only to caſt Sand into the Eyes of the People, and to labour, in ſome degree, to juſtifie himſelf in ſo ſtrange an action, and to devolve the Cauſe of it upon *Chah-Jehan*

Jehan and *Dara*, as if he had been forced to such proceedings. They are things, which are difficult enough well to discover. However it be, as soon as *Chah-Jehan* was shut up, almost all the *Omrahs* were in a manner necessitated to go and make their Court to *Aureng-Zebe* and *Morad-Bakche*; and (which is almost incredible) there was not one that had the courage to stir, or to attempt the least in the behalf of his King, and for him that had made them what they were, and raised them from the dust, and perhaps from slavery it self (which is ordinary enough in that Court) to advance them to Riches and Honour. Yet some few there are, as *Danechmend-Kan*, and some others, that took no side; but all the rest declared for *Aureng-Zebe*.

'Tis notwithstanding to be noted what I said, that they were necessitated to do what they did. For 'tis not in the *Indies*, as in *France*, or other States of *Christendom*, where the Grandees and Nobles have large Possessions of of Land, and great Revenues, which enables them for a while to subsist of themselves. There they have nothing but Pensions (as I have already touch'd above) which the King can take away from them at all hours, and thus ruin them in an instant; so that they shall be considered no more than if they never had been, nor have any credit to borrow a farthing.

Aureng-Zebe therefore having thus assured himself of *Chah-Jehan*, and of all the *Omrahs*, took what Sums of Money he thought fit out of the Treasury; and then having left *Chah-hest-Kan*, his Uncle, Governour of the Town, he went away with *Morad-Bakche* to pursue *Dara*.

The day that the Army was to march out of *Agra*, the particular Friends of *Morad-Bakche*, especially his Eunuch *Chah-Abas*, who knew, that the excess of civility and respect is ordinarily a sign of imposture, counselled him, that since he was King, and every body treated him with the Title of Majesty, and *Aureng-Zebe* himself

himself acknowledged him for such, he should let him go to pursue *Dara*, and stay himself with his Troops about *Agra* and *Dehli*. If he had followed this counsel, 'tis certain, that he would have embarassed *Aureng-Zebe* not a little; but 'twas fatal, that he should neglect so good advice: *Aureng-Zebe* is too fortunate; *Morad-Bakche* entirely confideth in his promises, and in the Oaths of Fidelity they had sworn to one another upon the Alcoran. They went away together, and went with the same pace towards *Dehli*.

When they were come to *Maturas*, three or four small days Journeys from *Agra*, the Friends of *Morad-Bakche*, who perceived something, endeavour'd again to perswade him, that he should beware; assuring him, that *Aureng-Zebe* had evil designs, and that beyond all doubt some mischief was upon the Anvil; that they had notice of it from all parts, and that by no means, for that day at least, he should go to see him; that it would be much

better

of the Empire of MOGOL.

better to prevent the stroke the soonest it might be; that he was only to forbear going to visit him that day, excusing himself with some indisposition. But whatsoever could be said to him, he believed nothing of it, his Ears were stopp'd to all the good advice that was given him, and as if he had been enchanted by the Friendship of *Aureng-Zebe*, he could not hold to go to him that very night, and to stay at Supper with him. As soon as he was come, *Aureng-Zebe*, who expected him, and had already prepared all things with *Mirkam*, and three or four of his most intimate Captains, was not wanting in embracements, and in redoubling his Courtship, civilities and submissions, in so much as gently to pass his handkerchief over his face, and to wipe off his sweat and dust, treating him still with the Title of King and Majesty. In the mean time, the Table is served, they sup, the conversation grows warm, they discourse of various things as they use to do; and at last there is brought a huge
Bottle

Bottle of excellent *Chiras* Wine, and some other Bottles of *Caboul* Wine, for a Debauch. Then *Aureng-Zebe*, as a grave serious Man, and one that would appear a great Mahumetan, and very regular, nimbly riseth from Table, and having with much kindness invited *Morad-Bakche*, who loved a Glass of Wine very well, and who relish'd the Wine that was served, scrupled not to drink of it to excess. In a word, he made himself drunk, and fell asleep. This was the thing that was wished; for presently some Servants of his that were there, were commanded away, under a pretence, to let him sleep without making any noise; and then his Zable and Ponyard were taken from about him: But *Aureng-Zebe* was not long, but came himself and waken'd him. He entred into the Chamber, and roughly hit him with his foot, and when he began to open a little his Eyes, he made to him this short and surprising Reprimand: What means this, *said he*, What shame and what ignominy is this,

this, that such a King as you are, should have so little temper, as thus to make himself drunk? What will be said both of you and me? Take this infamous Man, this Drunkard, tye him hand and foot, and throw him into that room to sleep out his Wine. No sooner said, but it was executed; notwithstanding all his appeal and out-cry, five or six persons fall upon him, and fetter his hands and feet. The things could not be done, but some of his Men that were thereabout had news of it. They made some noise, and would enter forcibly; but *Allah-Couly*, one of his chief Officers, and the Master of his Artillery, that had been gained long before, threatened them, and made them draw back. Without any delay, Men were sent through the whole Army to calm this first Commotion, which also might have proved dangerous; they made them believe it was nothing, they having been present, that *Morad-Bakche* was only drunk, that in that condition he had railed at every body, and

and *Aureng-Zebe* himself, i[n]
that there had been a neces[sity]
him drunk and furious, t[o]
apart; that the next day-[
see him abroad; after he h[ad]
his Wine. In the mean [time]
Presents walked about a[mongst]
mongst the chief Officers o[f]
their Pay was forthwith
they had great Promises m[ade]
and as there was none, th[e]
long since apprehended
thing, there was no great
see almost all things quiete[d]
morning; so that the very
this poor Prince was shut u[p]
close house, such an one as
be placed on Elephants to
men, and he was carried
Dehli into *Slimager*, which
old Fortress in the midst of [

After that all was thus
except the Eunuch *Chah-*[
caused difficulty enough, [
received the whole Army
Bakche into his Service, and
Dara, who marched apac[e]

Lahor, with an intention well to fortifie himſelf in that place, and thither to draw his Friends. But *Aureng-Zebe*, followed him with ſo much ſpeed, that he had not time to do any great matter, finding himſelf neceſſitated to retreat, and to take the way of *Multan*, where alſo he could do nothing conſiderable, becauſe that *Aureng-Zebe*, notwithſtanding the great heat, marched night and day; in ſo much, that to encourage all to make haſte, he ſometimes advanced almoſt all alone two or three leagues before the whole Army, finding himſelf often obliged to drink ill water like others, to be content with a cruſt of dry bread, and to ſleep under a Tree, ſtaying for his Army in the midſt of the high-way, laying his Head on his Shield like a common Souldier. So that *Dara* found himſelf conſtrained to abandon *Multan* alſo, that he might avoid being near *Aureng-Zebe*, whom he was not able to encounter. Here 'tis that the Stateſmen of this Country have reaſoned very diverſly: For 'tis ſaid,

said, that if *Dara*, when he went out of *Lahor*, had cast himself into the Kingdom of *Caboul*, as he was advised, he would there have found above ten thousand warlike Men, designed against the *Augans*, the *Persians*, and the *Usbecs*, and for a Guard to that Country, the Governour whereof was *Mohabet-Kan*, one of the most potent and the most ancient of *Indostan*, and that had never been *Aureng-Zebe*'s Friend; that, besides, he would have been there at the Gate of *Persia* and *Usbec*; that it was likely, that there being no want of Money, all that *Militia*, and *Mohabet-Kan* himself, would have embraced his Party, and that further he might have drawn assistance, not only from *Usbec*, but also from *Persia*, as well as from *Houmayon*, whom the *Persians* had restored to his Country against *Zaber-Kan*, King of the *Patans*, who had driven him thence. But *Dara* was too unfortunate to follow so good advice. Instead of that he went towards *Scimdy*, to cast himself into the Fortress of *Tatabakar*,

bakar, that strong and famous place, seated in the midst of the River *Indus*.

Aureng-Zebe seeing him take this way, found it not fit to follow him further off, being extremely glad that he had not taken the way to *Caboul*. He contented himself to send after him seven or eight thousand Men, under the Conduct of *Mir-baba*, his Foster-brother, and turned back with the same expedition to the place whence he was come, much apprehending lest any thing should fall out about *Agra*; lest some or other of those potent *Raja's*, as *Jesseigne*, or *Jessomseigne*, should make an attempt in his absence, to free *Chah-Jehan* out of Prison; or lest *Soliman Chekouh*, together with the *Raja* of *Serenaguer*, should descend from the Hills; or lest also *Sultan Sujah* should approach too near *Agra*. Behold a little accident, which one day befel him, for too great precipitation.

When he thus returned from *Multan* towards *Labor*, and marched his ordinary swift pace, he saw the *Raja*

Jes-

Jesseigne come against him, accompanied with four or five thousand of his *Ragipous*, in a very good equipage; *Aureng-Zebe*, who had left his Army behind, and who also knew that this *Raja* was very affectionate to *Chah-Jehan*, was sufficiently surprised, as may easily be imagined, fearing lest this *Raja* should make use of this occasion, and do a Master-piece of State, by seizing on him, to draw *Chah-Jehan* out of Prison, which at that time was very easie to do. Neither is it known, whether this *Raja* had not some such design; for he had marched with extraordinary speed, in so much that *Aureng-Zebe* had no news of it, believing him yet to be at *Dehli*. But what may not resolution and presence of mind do? *Aureng-Zebe*, without any alteration of his countenance, marched directly towards the *Raja*, and as far off as he could see him, maketh signs to him with his hands, importing that he should make hast to a nearer approach, crying out to him with a loud voice, *Salamed Bached Rajagi*,

of the Empire of MOGOL.

jagi, *Salamed Bached Babagi*, treating him with the Titles of *Lord Raja* and *Lord Father*. When the *Raja* was come to him; I expected you, *said he*, with great impatience; the Work is done, *Dara* is loft, he is all alone; I have sent *Mir-baba* after him, from whom he cannot escape: And for an excess of kindness to him, he took off his Necklace of Pearls, and put it about the Neck of this *Raja*: And the sooner to rid himself handsomely of him, (for he wish'd him far enough) Go, *saith he*, with all the expedition you can to *Lahor*, my Army is somewhat tyred; go quickly to attend me there; I apprehend that else something sinister might fall out there; I make you Governour of that place, and put all things into your hands. For the rest, I am exceedingly obliged to you for what you have done with *Soliman Chekouh*: Where have you left *Delil-Kan*? I shall find my revenge of him. Make all possible dispatch, *Salamed Bached*, Farewell.

Dara being arrived at *Tata-bakar*, made

made Governour of that place a very understanding, gallant, and generous Eunuch, with a very good Garrison of *Patans* and *Sayeds*; and for Cannoneers, a good number of *Franguis*, *Portugals*, *English*, *French*, and *Germans*, who had follow'd him out of great hopes he had given them, (for, if his Affairs had prospered, and he were become King, we must all have resolved to be *Omrahs*, as many *Franguis* as we were.) He there left also the greatest part of his Treasure; he wanted as yet no Gold nor Silver; and staying there but a very few days, he marched away with two or three thousand Men only, descending along the River *Indus* towards *Scindy*, and from thence crossing with an incredible celerity all those Territories of the *Raja Katche*, he arrived in *Guzaratte*, and came to the Gates of *Amadevat*. The Father-in-law of *Aureng-Zebe*, called *Chah-Navaze-Kan*, was Governour there, with a very good Garrison, able to resist. Yet notwithstanding, whether it was that he

of the Empire of MOGOL.

he was surprised, or that he wanted courage, (for although he was of those ancient Princes of *Machate*, yet he was no great Souldier, though a Man of a very obliging and civil conversation) he did not oppose *Dara*, but rather received him very honourably, and even managed him afterwards with so much dexterity, that *Dara* was so simple as to trust himself with him, and to communicate to him his Designs; in so much as that he shew'd him the Letters which he received from the *Raja Jessomseigne*, and of many other of his Friends, which prepared themselves to come to him; although it proved too true, what every body told him, and his Friends confirmed by Letters, that certainly this *Chah-Navaze-Kan* would betray him.

Never was any Man more surprised than *Aureng-Zebe*, when he heard that *Dara* was in *Amadevat*: For he well knew, that he wanted no Money, and that all his Friends, and all the discontented Party, which was numerous, would not fail to betake themselves by
little

little and little to him: And on the other side, he found it not safe to go and find him out himself in that place, by removing himself so far from *Agra* and *Chah-Jehan*, to go and embarass himself in all those Countries of the *Raja's*, *Jesseigne*, *Jessomseigne*, and others, that are in those Provinces. Besides he apprehended, lest *Sultan Sujah* should advance with a strong Army, which was already about *Elabas*, and left the *Raja* of *Serenaguer* should descend from the Hills with *Soliman Chekouh*: So that he was sufficiently perplexed and troubled, not knowing which way to turn. At last he believed it best, to leave *Dara* for a time quiet where he was, and to go thither where his presence and Army was most necessary, which was towards *Sultan Sujah*, who had already passed the River *Ganges* at *Elabas*.

This *Sultan Sujah* was come to encamp in a little Village called *Kadjoue*, and had conveniently seized himself of a great *Talab*, or Reservatory of Water, which is there in the way; and

and *Aureng-Zebe* came to place himself on the side of a small Torrent, at the distance of a mile and an half from thence, on *Agra's* side. Between both was a very fair Campagne, very proper for a Battel. *Aureng-Zebe* was no sooner arrived, but being impatient to end this War, at break of day he went to face *Sujah*, leaving his Baggage on the other side of the Torrent. He fell upon *Sujah* with an effort unimaginable. *Emir-Jemla*, Prisoner of of *Decan*, and who arrived just on the day of the Combat, fearing *Dara* no more, because his Family was more in safety, did there also lay out all his force, courage, and dexterity. But seeing that *Sultan Sujah* had well fortified himself, and was accompanied with a very good Artillery, advantagiously placed, it was not possible for *Aureng-Zebe* to force him, nor to make him retreat from thence, so as to make him lose those Waters. On the contrary, he was obliged himself to draw back several times, so vigorously was he repulsed, in so much that

that he found himself in great perplexity. *Sultan Sujah* not being willing to advance too far into the Campagne, nor to remove from that advantagious place where he was, pretending only to defend himself; which was very prudently done. For he foresaw, that *Aureng-Zebe* could not stay there long, and that in that hot season he would be absolutely obliged to turn back towards the Torrent for the Water; and that, when he should do so, he would fall upon his Rear. *Aureng-Zebe* also foresaw well enough the same thing, and that was the reason why he was so forward and pressing; but behold another more troublesome accident.

In this very time he receiveth intelligence, that the *Raja Jessomseigne*, who in *appearance* had accommodated himself with him, was fallen upon his Rear, and plunder'd his Baggage and Treasure. This News astonished him much, and the more, because he perceived that his Army which had heard of it was thereby frighted, and

fallen

of the Empire of MOGOL.

fallen into diforder. Yet he lofes not his judgment for all this; and being well aware, that to turn back was to hazard all, he refolved, as in the Battel of *Dara*, to bear up the beft he could, and to expect with a fteady foot all Events. In the mean time, the diforder grew worfe and worfe in his Army: *Sujah*, who was refolved to profit of the occafion, taketh his time, and preffeth him vigoroufly. He that led *Aureng-Zebe*'s Elephant is killed with the fhot of an Arrow; he leads the Beaft as well as he can himfelf, 'till another could be had in that Leaders place. Arrows rain upon him; he returns many himfelf, his Elephant begins to be frighted, and to go back. Behold him now in great extremity, and brought to that point, that one foot of his was out of the feat, as if he meant to caft himfelf to the ground; and no Man knows what in that trouble he had not done, if *Emir-Jemla*, being nigh, and performing, like a Great Man as he was, beyond imagination, called to him,

in

in holding up his hand, *Decan-kou*, *Decan-kou*, where is *Decan*? This seems to have been the greatest extremity, to which *Aureng-Zebe* could be reduced. One would have said, 'twas now and here that Fortune had abandon'd him, and there is almost no appearance of a possibility to escape. But his good Fortune is stronger than all that: *Sultan Sujah* must be routed, and take flight, like *Dara*, to save his life: *Aureng-Zebe* must remain victorious, carry away the Bell, and be King of the *Indies*.

We are to remember the Battel of *Samonguer*, and that, in appearance, slight accident which ruined *Dara*: 'Tis the same over-sight, or rather the same Treason, which is now destroying *Sultan Sujah*. One of his chief Captains, *Allah-verdi-Kan*, who (as some say) had been gained, useth the same Artifice that *Calil-ullah-Kan* had employ'd towards *Dara*; though there were some who believed, that there was no malice in the case, and that it was a meer piece of flattery.

For

of the Empire of MOGOL. 125
For seeing that the whole Army of *Aureng-Zebe* was in disorder, he ran towards *Sultan Sujah*, telling him the same thing, that *Calil-ullah-Kan* did to *Dara*, and begging of him with folded hands, that he would stay no longer in so great danger upon his Elephant. Come down, *said he*, in the Name of God, mount on Horse-back, God hath made you Soveraign of the *Indies*, let us pursue those Fugitives, let not *Aureng-Zebe* escape us.

But not to stay long from declaring the strange Fortune of *Aureng-Zebe*, and the incredible conjuncture that recovers his desperate condition; *Sultan Sujah*, not more considerate than *Dara*, commits the same Fault; and he was no sooner come down from his Elephant, but his Army seeing him no more, was struck with a terrour, believing there was Treason, and that he was either taken or slain. Whereupon they disbanded without any more ado, as *Dara*'s Army did in the Battel of *Samonguer*; and the Defeat was so great, that the *Sultan* was
for-

fortunate in that he could save himself.

Jessomseigne hearing this unexpected news, and perceiving it was not very safe for him to tarry there, contented himself with the Spoil he had got, and with all diligence marched streight to *Agra*, thence to pass to his Countrey. The noise was already in *Agra*, that *Aureng-Zebe* had lost the Battel, that he was taken, together with *Emir-Jemla*, and that *Sultan Sujah* brought them both Prisoners. In so much, that *Chah-hest-Kan*, who was Governour of the Town, and Uncle to *Aureng-Zebe*, seeing *Jessomseigne*, whose Treachery he had heard of, at the Gates, and despairing of his Life, had taken into his hand a Cup of Poyson to make himself away, and had, as they say, in very deed swallowed it, if his Women had not fallen upon him and hindred him: So that 'tis thought, if *Jessomseigne* had had the wit and courage to stay longer in *Agra*, if he had threatened boldly, and promised and acted vigorously for

the

the freedom of *Chah-Jehan*, he might have drawn him out of prison; so much the more easily, because all *Agra* was for two whole days in that belief, that *Aureng-Zebe* was overcome. But *Jessomseigne*, who knew how all things went, and who durst not long stay there, nor attempt any thing, did nothing but pass, returning with all speed homewards.

Aureng-Zebe, who apprehended mischief from *Agra*, and fear'd left *Jessomseigne* should undertake something for *Chah-Jehan*, was not long in the pursuit after *Sultan Sujah*; he turn'd short for *Agra* with his whole Army, where he staid a good while, giving order for all things. Mean time he received intelligence, that *Sultan Sujah* had not lost many Men in his being routed, for want of farther pursuit; that also from the Lands of the *Raja's*, which are in those quarters, on the right and left of *Ganges*, he raised great Forces, upon the score of the reputation he had of being very rich, and very liberal, and that he fortified himself

self in *Elabas*, that important and famous Passage of *Ganges*, which with its Fortress is the first In-let into *Bengale*. And then he considered also, that he had about him two Persons, which indeed were very capable to serve him, *Sultan Mahmoud* his Eldest Son, and *Emir-Jemla* ; but he well knew, that those who have done good service to their Prince, grow often insolent, in the belief, that all is due to them, and that they cannot be recompenced enough. He perceived already, that the former of them began very much to emancipate himself, and that every day he became more arrogant, for having seized on the Fortress of *Agra*, and by that means had broken all the Designs which *Chah-Jehan* could have formed. And as to the *latter*, he knew indeed the force of his Understanding, his Conduct, and Valour; but that was the very thing which made him apprehend him the more: For knowing that he was very rich, that his reputation was great, that he passed for the *First Mover* in

Affairs,

of the Empire of MOGOL.

Affairs, and for the ableft Man in all the *Indies*, he doubted not, but that after the Example of *Sultan Mahmond*, he entertain'd himfelf with big hopes. All this certainly would have been able to perplex an ordinary Spirit, but *Aureng-Zebe* found a Remedy to all. He knew to remove them both with fo much prudence, and even with fo much handfomnefs, that neither of them found any caufe to complain of it. He fent them both againft *Sultan Sujah* with a puiffant Army, letting *Emir* fecretly know, that the Government of *Bengale*, which is the beft quarter of *Indoftan*, was defign'd for him, to hold it during his life, and for his Son after his deceafe; and that thereby he would begin to exprefs to him his acknowledgments for the great Services he had done him; and that therefore it belonged only to him to defeat *Sujah*, and that as foon as he fhould have compaffed it, he would make him *Mir-ul Omrahs*, which is the firft and the moft honourable place of *Indoftan*, and no lefs than the Prince of the *Omrahs*. K To

To *Sultan Mahmoud*, his Son, he said only thefe few words: Remember that thou art the Eldeft of my Children, that 'tis for thy felf thou goeft forth to fight; that thou haft done much, but yet nothing, if thou overcomeft not *Sujah*, who is our greateft and powerfulleft Enemy; I hope, God affifting me, to be foon Mafter of the reft.

With thefe words he difmiffed them both, with ordinary honours, that is, with rich Vefts, fome Horfes and Elephants gallantly harneffed; making in the mean time *Emir-Jemla* to confent, that his only Son, *Mahmet-Emir-Kan*, fhould ftay with him for a good Education, or rather for a Pledge of his Fidelity; and *Sultan Mahmoud*, that his Wife fhould remain in *Agra* (which was the Daughter of the above-mention'd King of *Golkonda*) as too troublefome a thing in an Army, and in fuch an Expedition.

Sultan Sujah, who was always in the apprehenfion, left the *Raja's* of the lower *Bengale*, which he had ill treated, fhould should be raised against him, and who feared nothing more than to have to do with *Emir-Jemla*, had no sooner received this News; but apprehending that the passage to *Bengale* would be obstructed, and that *Emir* would pass in some other place the River *Ganges*, either lower or higher than *Elabas*, raised his Camp, and went down to *Benares* and *Patna*, whence he betook himself to *Mogiere*, a small Town seated upon the *Ganges*; a place commonly call'd the *Key* of the Kingdom of *Bengale*, being a kind of Streight between the Mountains and the Woods, which are not far from thence. He thought fit to stay in that place, and there to fortifie himself; and for greater safety, he caused a great Trench to be made, which I have seen, passing that way some years after, from the Town and River unto the Mountain, being well resolved there to attend *Emir-Jemla*, and to dispute that passage with him. But he was sufficiently astonish'd, when he was told, that the Troops of *Emir*, which

which flowly defcended along the River *Ganges*, were certainly for nothing but to amufe him; that himfelf was not there; that he had gained the *Raja's* of thofe Mountains, which are on the right hand of the River; and that he and *Sultan Mahmoud* marched apace over their Lands with all the Flower of the Army, drawing ftraight to *Rage-Mehalle*, to intercept him: So that he was conftrained to quit, as foon as he could, his Fortifications; yet notwithftanding he made fo much hafte, that though he was obliged to follow thofe windings, which the River *Ganges* on that fide maketh toward the left hand, he prevented *Emir* by fome days, and arrived firft at *Rage-Mehalle*, where he had time to fortifie himfelf; becaufe *Emir* having heard this News, took his March to the left hand towards *Ganges*, through very ill ways, there to expect his Troops, which came down with the Body of the Artillery and the Baggage along the River. As foon as all was come, he went to attaque *Sultan Sujah*, who

defen-

of the Empire of MOGOL. 133
defended himself very well for five or six days; but seeing that the Artillery of *Emir*, which played incessantly, ruined all his Fortifications, which were made but of sandy Earth and Faggots, and that he could not but with much difficulty make resistance in that place, besides that the Season of the Rain began, he retired himself, at the favour of the night, leaving behind two great Peeces of Cannon. *Emir* durst not follow him in the night, for fear of some Ambush, putting off the pursuit 'till the next morning: But *Sujah* had the good luck, that at the break of day there began to fall a Rain, which lasted above three days; so that *Emir* could not only not stir out of *Rage-Mehalle*, but saw himself obliged to pass the Winter there, by reason of the excessive Rains in that Country, which render the ways so troublesome for more than four months, *viz. July*, *August*, *September*, and *October*, that the Armies cannot possibly march. And hereby *Sultan Sujah* had the means to retire himself, and to chuse what
K 3   place

place he would, having time enough to fortifie his Army, and to send out of the inferiour *Bengale* for many Peeces of Cannon, and a good number of *Portugals*, that were retired thither, because of the great fertility of the Countrey: For he much courted all those *Portugal* Fathers, Missionaries, that are in that Province, promising them no less than that he would make them all rich, and build Churches for them wheresoever they would. And they were indeed capable to serve him, it being certain, that in the Kingdom of *Bengale* there are to be found no less than eight or nine thousand Families of *Franguis*, *Portugals*, and these either Natives or Mesticks.

But *Sultan Mahmoud*, who for the reason above-mentioned was grown fierce, and aspired perhaps to greater things than at that time he ought, did pretend to command the Army absolutely, and that *Emir-Jemla* should follow his Orders, letting also from time to time fall insolent words in reference to his Father *Aureng-Zebe*, as if if he were obliged to him for the Crown, and uttering Expreſſions of contempt and threat againſt *Emir-Jemla*; which cauſed great coldneſs betwixt them two, which laſted a pretty while, until *Sultan Mahmoud* underſtood, that his Father was very much diſſatisfied with his conduct: And apprehending, leſt *Emir* had order to ſeize on his perſon, he went away to *Sultan Sujah*, accompanied with a very ſmall number, and to him he made great promiſes, and ſwore fidelity. But *Sujah*, who feared *Aureng-Zebe* and *Emir-Jemla*'s ſnares, could not truſt him, having always an Eye upon his Actions, without giving him any conſiderable Command; which he ſo diſguſted, that ſome months after, not knowing what would become of him, he left *Sultan Sujah*, and returned to *Emir*, who received him well enough, aſſuring him, that he would write in his behalf to *Aureng-Zebe*, and do his utmoſt to make him forget that fault.

I think fit here to take notice, on

the

the by, of what many have told me, *viz,* That this Escape of *Sultan Mahmoud* was altogether made by the Artifices of *Aureng-Zebe*, who cared not much to hazard this Son of his to try to destroy *Sujah*, and who was glad enough, that whatever the Event were, he might have a specious pretence to put him in a place of surety. However it be, he afterwards shew'd himself much dissatisfied with him, and wrote to him a severe Letter, in which he enjoyn'd him to return to *Dehli*, but giving order in the mean time, that he should not come so far: For he no sooner had passed the River *Ganges*, but he met with Troops that stopp'd him, and put him up in a small Chair, (as was done to *Morad-Bakche*) and carried him to *Goualeor*, whence 'tis thought he will never be set at liberty: *Aureng-Zebe* by this means freeing himself from great perplexity; who then also let his second Son, *Sultan Mazum*, know, that the point of Reigning is so delicate a thing, that Kings must be jealous even of their own

of the Empire of MOGOL. 137
own shadow; adding, that if he be
not discreet, the like may befall him
what had befallen his Brother, and
that he ought to think *Aureng-Zebe*
was not a Man, that would suffer that
to be done to himself, what *Chah-Jehan* did to his Father *Jehan-Guyre*,
and what he had also lately seen done
to *Chah-Jehan*.

And indeed we may on this occasion
say, that if this Son continue to behave himself as he hath done hitherto,
Aureng-Zebe will have no cause to
suspect him, and to be dissatisfied with
him: For no Slave can be more tractable, and *Aureng-Zebe* himself never
appear'd more careless of Greatness,
nor more given to Devotion than he:
Yet I have known Men of Parts, who
believed, that he is not so in good
earnest, but by superlative policy and
craft, like that of his Father, which
we may have the proof of in time.

Whilst all these things were thus
transacted in *Bengale*, and that *Sultan
Sujah* resisted the best he could the
Forces of *Emir-Jemla*, passing now

on

on one side of the River *Ganges*, of a Channel, or some other River, (for that Countrey is full of them) then on the other; *Aureng-Zebe* kept himself about *Agra*, going to and fro; and at length, after he had also sent *Morad-Bakche* to *Gowaleor*, he came to *Dehli*, where in good earnest he took upon him publickly to act the King, giving order for all Affairs of the Kingdom, and especially thinking on means to catch *Dara*, and to get him out of *Guzaratte*, which was a very hard thing, for the Reasons already mentioned. But the great good Fortune, and the singular dexterity of *Aureng-Zebe* soon drew him thence; which now follows next to be related.

Jessomseigne, who had retired himself to his Countrey, and made the best of what he had taken in the Battel of *Kadjoue*, raised a strong Army, and wrote to *Dara*, that he should come to *Agra* as soon as he could, and that he would joyn with his Forces. *Dara*, who had by this time set on foot a
pretty

of the Empire of MOGOL. 139
pretty numerous Army (though it consisted, for the most part, but of gathered people) and who hoped, that approaching to *Agra*, many of his old Friends, seeing him with *Jessomseigne*, would not fail to joyn with him also, immediately leaveth *Amadevad*, and marcheth with great speed to *Asmire*, seven or eight days journey from *Agra*. But *Jessomseigne* kept not his word with him: The *Raja Jesseigne* interposed to make his peace with *Aureng-Zebe*, and to fasten him to his Party; or, at least, to hinder his Design, which was capable to ruin himself, and to make all the *Raja's* rise; and wrote to him several Letters, giving him to understand the great danger he went to expose himself to, by espousing a Party in that extremity, as that of *Dara's* was; that he should well consider what he was going to do; that he went about wholly to destroy himself, and all his whole Family; that *Aureng-Zebe* would never forgive him; that he was a *Raja* as himself; that he should think on sparing

ring the blood of the *Ragipous*; that if he thought to draw the *Raja's* to his Party, he would find those that would hinder him from it. In a word, that it was a business which concern'd all the Gentry of *Indostan*, and exposed them to danger, if way were given to kindle a Fire, which would not be extinguish'd at pleasure. And lastly, if he would leave *Dara* to himself, *Aureng-Zebe* would forget all that had passed, and present him with all he had taken, and give him that very instant the Government of *Guzaratte*, which would be very convenient for him, that Countrey being near his Lands; that he could be there in full liberty and safety, and as long as he pleased, and that himself would be Caution for all. In a word, this *Raja* acted his part so well, that he made *Jessomseigne* return to his Land, whilst *Aureng-Zebe* approached with his whole Army to *Asmire*, and encamped in the sight of that of *Dara*.

And now what could this poor Prince *Dara* do? He seeth himself aban-

of the Empire of MOGOL.

abandoned, and fruſtrated of his hopes. He conſiders, that to turn back ſafe to *Amadevad* was impoſſible, in regard that it was a March of thirty and five days; that it was in the heart of Summer; that water would fail him; that they were all the Lands of *Raja's*, Friends or Allies of *Jeſſeigne* or *Jeſſomſeigne*; that the Army of *Aureng-Zebe*, which was not haraſſed like his, would not fail to follow him. 'Tis as good, *ſaith he*, to periſh here; and although the Match be altogether unequal, let us venture all, and give Battel once more. But alas! what does he mean to do? He is not only abandoned by all, but he hath yet with him *Chah-Navaze-Kan*, whom he truſts, and who betrays him, and diſcovers all his Deſigns to *Aureng-Zebe*. 'Tis true, that *Chah-Navaze-Kan* was puniſh'd for his perfidiouſneſs, and killed in the Battel, whether it was by the hands of *Dara* himſelf, as many told me, or (which is more probable) by ſome of *Aureng-Zebe's* Army, who being ſecret Partiſans of *Dara*, found

found means to get to him, and to dispatch him, fearing left he should discover them, and have some knowledge of the Letters they had written to *Dara*: But what did it benefit him at that time, that *Chah-Navaze-Kan* was dead? *Dara* should have sooner follow'd the advice of his Friends, and never have confided in him.

The Fight began between Nine and Ten of the Clock in the morning: *Dara*'s Artillery, which was very well placed on a little eminency, was loud enough; but, as was said, most of the Peeces without Bullets; so was he betray'd by all! 'Tis needless to relate the other particulars of this Battel; it was properly not a Battel, but a Rout. I shall only say, that hardly the Onset was begun, but *Jesseigne* was near and in sight of *Dara*, to whom he sent word, that he should fly presently, unless he would be taken. So that this poor Prince, being altogether surprised, was constrained to run away instantly, and with so much disorder and precipitation, that he had not
leisure

leisure to put up his Baggage. It was no small matter, that he was able to get away with his Wife, and the rest of his Family. And 'tis certain, that if the *Raja Jesseigne* would have done what he could, he could never have escaped; but he always had a respect to the Royal Family; or rather, he was too crafty and politick, and had too great forecast, to venture to lay hands on a Prince of the Blood.

This unfortunate Prince, deserted by almost all, and finding himself accompanied but of two thousand Men at most, was forced in the hottest of Summer to cross, without Tents or Baggage, all those Countries of the *Raja's*, that are almost from *Asmire* to *Amadevad*. Mean time the *Koullis*, which are the Countrey People, and the worst of all the *Indies*, and the greatest Robbers, follow him night and day, rifle and kill his Souldiers, with so much cruelty, that no Man could stay two hundred paces behind the Body, but he was presently stripp'd naked, or butcher'd upon the least

resi-

resistance. Yet notwithstanding, *Dara* made shift to get near *Amadevad*, when he hoped, that the next day, or soon after, he should enter into the Town to refresh himself, and to try once more to gather again some Forces: But all things fall out contrary to vanquished and unfortunate Men.

 The Governour, whom he had left in the Castle of *Amadevad*, had already received both menacing and promising Letters from *Aureng-Zebe*, which made him lose courage, and incline to that side; in so much that he wrote to *Dara*, forbidding him to come nearer, if he did, he would find the Gates shut, and all in Arms.

 Three days before I met this unhappy Prince, by a strange accident, when he obliged me to follow him; having no Physitian about him; and the night before that he received this News from the Governour of *Amadevad*, he did me the favour to make me come into the *Karavan-Serrak* where he was, fearing lest the *Koullis* should assassinate me: And (what is hard enough

enough to believe in *Indostan*, where the Grandees especially are so jealous of their Wives) I was so near to the Wife of this Prince, that the Cords of the *Kanates*, or Wind-screen, which enclosed them (for they had not so much as a poor Tent) were fastened to the Wheels of my Chariot. I relate this circumstance by the by only, to shew the extremity *Dara* was reduced to.

When these Women heard this sad news (which was at the break of day, as I well remember) they broke out upon a sudden into such strange cryes and lamentations, that they forced tears from ones Eyes. And now behold all was in an unexpressible confusion: Every one looks upon his neighbour, and no body knows what to do, or what will become of him. Soon after we saw *Dara* come forth, half dead, now speaking to one, then another, even to the meanest Souldiers. He seeth all astonish'd, and ready to abandon him. What counsel? whither can he go? he must be gone instantly. You may

may judge of the extremity he must needs be in, by this small accident I am going to mention. Of three great Oxen of *Guzaratte*, which I had for my Chariot, one died the night before, another was dying, and the third was tyred out (for we had been forced to march for three days together, almost night and day, in an intolerable heat and dust:) Whatever *Dara* could say or command, whether he alledged it was for himself, or for one of his Women that was hurt in her Leg, or for me; he could not possibly procure for me, whether Oxe, or Camel, or Horse: So that he was obliged, to my good fortune, to leave me there. I saw him march away, and that with tears in his Eyes, accompanied with four or five hundred Cavaliers at most, and with two Elephants, that were said to be laden with Gold and Silver; and I heard them say, that they were to take their march towards *Tatabakar*; for he had no other Game to play, though even that seem'd in a manner impossible,

con-

considering the small number of people left him, and the great sandy Desarts to be waded through in the hottest season, most of them without water fit to drink. And indeed most of those that follow'd him, and even divers of his Women, did there perish, either of drought, or the unwholesome waters, or the tiresome ways and ill food, or lastly, because stripped by the *Koullis* above-mention'd. Yet notwithstanding all this, *Dara* made hard shift to get to the *Raja Katche*; unhappy even herein, that he perish'd not himself in this March.

This *Raja* at first gave him a very good reception, even so far as to promise him assistance with all his Forces, provided he would give his Daughter in Marriage to his Son. But *Jesseigne* soon wrought as much with this *Raja*, as he had done with *Jessomseigne*. So that *Dara* one day seeing the kindness of this Barbarian cooled upon a sudden, and that consequently his Person was in danger there, he betakes himself to the pursuit of his Expedition to *Tatabakar*.

To relate how I got away from those Robbers, the *Koullis*, in what manner I moved them to compassion, how I saved the best part of my small Treasure, how we became good friends by the means of my profession of Physick, my Servants (perplexed as well as my self) swearing that I was the greatest Physitian of the World, and that the People of *Dara*, at their going away, had ill treated me, and taken from me all my best things: How, after having kept me with them seven or eight days, they had so much kindness and generosity, as to lend me an Oxe, and to conduct me so far, that I was in sight of *Amadevad*: And lastly, how from thence after some days I returned to *Dehli*, having lighted on an occasion to go with a certain *Omrah* passing thither; in which Journey I met from time to time, on the way, with Carkasses of Men, Elephants, Oxen, Horses, and Camels, the remainder of that unfortunate Army of *Dara*. These are things, I say, I must not insist upon to describe them.

Whilst

Whilft *Dara* advanced towards *Tatabakar*, the War continues in *Bengale*, and much longer than was believed, *Sultan Sujah* putting forth his utmoft, and playing his laft Game againft *Emir-Jemla*: Yet this did not much trouble *Aureng-Zebe*, who knew 'twas a great way between *Bengale* and *Agra*, and was fufficiently convinced of the prudence and valour of *Emir-Jemla*. That which difquieted him much more was, that he faw *Soliman Chekouh* fo near (for from *Agra* to the Mountains 'tis but eight days journey) whom he could not mafter, and who perpetually allarm'd him by the rumours that went continually about, as if he were coming down the Mountains with the *Raja*. 'Tis certainly very hard to draw him thence: But behold how he manages the matter to compafs it.

He maketh the *Raja Jeffeigne* write one Letter after another to the *Raja* of *Serenaguer*, promifing him very great things; if he would furrender *Soliman Chekouh* to him, and menacing

War at the same time, if he should obstinately keep him. The *Raja* answers, that he would rather lose his Estate, than do so unworthy an action. And *Aureng-Zebe*, seeing his resolution, taketh the Field, and marcheth directly to the foot of the Hills, and with an infinite number of Pike-men causeth the Rocks to be cut, and the passage to be widen'd. But the *Raja* laughs at all that; neither hath he much cause to fear on that side. *Aureng-Zebe* may cut long enough, they are Mountains inaccessible to an Army, and stones would be sufficient to stop the Forces of four *Indostans*; so that he was constrained to turn back again.

Dara in the mean time approacheth to the Fortress of *Tatabakar*, and when he was but two or three days journey off, he received News, that *Mir-baba*, who had long held it besieged, had at length reduced it to extremity: As I afterwards learned of our *French*, and other *Franguis* that were there, a pound of Rice and Meat having cost

there

of the Empire of MOGOL. 151

there above a Crown, and so of other Victuals in proportion: Yet the Governour held out; made Sallies, which extremely incommoded the Enemy; and shew'd all possible prudence, courage, and fidelity; deriding the endeavours of the General, *Mir-baba*, and all the menaces and promises of *Aureng-Zebe*.

And this also I learned afterwards of my Countrey-men, the *French*, and of all those other *Franguis* that were with him; who added, that when he heard that *Dara* was not far off, he redoubled his liberalities, and knew so well to gain the hearts of all his Souldiers, and to encourage them to do bravely, that there was not one of them, that was not resolved to sally out upon the Enemy, and to hazard all to raise the Siege, and to make *Dara* enter; and that he also knew so well to cast fear and terrour into the Camp of *Mir-baba*, by sending Spies about very cunningly to assure, that they had seen *Dara* approach with great resolution, and very good Forces;

that if he had come, as was believed he would do every moment, the Army of the Enemy was for disbanding upon his appearance, and even in part to go over to him. But he is still too unfortunate, to undertake any thing prosperously. Believing therefore, that to raise the Siege with such an handful of Men as he had was impossible, he did deliberate to pass the River *Indus*, and to endeavour to get into *Persia*; although that also would have had mighty difficulties and inconveniencies, by reason of the Desarts, and the small quantity of good waters in those parts; besides, that upon those Frontiers there are but mean *Rajas* and *Patans*, who acknowledge neither the *Persian* nor the *Mogol*. But his Wife did very much diswade him from it, for this weak reason, that he must, if he did so, expect to see his Wife and Daughter Slaves of the King of *Persia*; that that was a thing altogether unworthy of the Grandeur of his Family, and 'twas better to dye, than to undergo this infamy.

Dara,

Dara, being in great perplexity, remembred, that there was thereabout a certain *Patan*, powerful enough, called *Gion-Kan*, whose Life he had formerly saved twice, when *Chah-Jehan* had commanded he should be cast under the feet of an Elephant, for having rebelled divers times: He resolved to go to him, hoping that he could give him sufficient Succours to raise the Siege of *Tatabakar*; making account, that thence he would take his Treasure, and that going from thence, and gaining *Kandahar*, he could cast himself into the Kingdom of *Caboul*, having great hopes of *Mohabet-Kan*, who was Governour of it, because he was both potent and valiant, well beloved of his Countrey, and had obtained this Government by his (*Dara*'s) favour. But his Grandchild, *Sepe-Chekouh*, yet but very young, seeing his design, cast himself at his Feet, intreating him for God's sake, not to enter into the Countrey of that *Patan*. His Wife and Daughter did the same, remonstrating to him,

him, that he was a Robber, a revolted Governour, that he would infallibly betray him; that he ought not to stand upon the raising of the Siege, but rather endeavour to gain *Caboul*, that the thing was not impossible, forasmuch as *Mir-baba* was not like to quit the Siege to follow him, and to hinder him from getting thither.

Dara, being carried head-long by the force of his unhappy Destiny, rejected this counsel, and would hearken to nothing of what was proposed to him, saying, as was true, that the March would be very difficult, and very dangerous; and maintaining alwayes, that *Gion-Kan* would not be so mean, as to betray him, after all the good he had done him. He departed, notwithstanding all that could be said to him, and went to prove, at the price of his Life, That no trust is to be given to a wicked Man.

This Robber, who at first believed that he had numerous Troops following him, gave him the fairest reception that could be, and entertained
him

him with very great kindnefs and civility in appearance, placing his Souldiers here and there among his Subjects, with a ſtrict order to treat them well, and to give them what refreſhments the Countrey afforded: But when he found that he had not above two or three hundred Men in all, he quickly ſhow'd what he was. It is not known, whether he had not received ſome Letters from *Aureng-Zebe*, or whether his avarice had not been tempted by ſome Mules ſaid to be laden with Gold; which was all that could be ſaved hitherto, as well from the hands of Robbers, as of thoſe that conveyed it. Whatever it be, on a certain morning, when no body looked for any ſuch thing, all being taken up with the care of refreſhing themſelves, and believing all to be ſafe; behold this Traitor, who had beſtirr'd himſelf all night to get armed Men from all parts, fell upon *Dara* and *Sepe-Chekouh*, killed ſome of their Men that ſtood up to defend themſelves; forgot not to ſeize on the loads of the Mules,

Mules, and of all the Jewels of the Women; made *Dara* to be tyed faſt upon an Elephant, commanding the Executioner to ſit behind, and to cut off his head upon the leaſt ſign given, in caſe he ſhould be ſeen to reſiſt, or that any one ſhould attempt to deliver him. And in this ſtrange poſture he was carried to the Army before *Tatabakar*, where he put him into the hands of *Mir-baba*, the General, who cauſed him to be conducted in the company of this ſame Traitor to *Lahor*, and thence to *Dehli*.

When he was at the Gates of *Dehli*, it was deliberated by *Aureng-Zebe*, whether he ſhould be made to paſs through the midſt of the City, or no, to carry him thence to *Goualeor*. Many did adviſe, that that was by no means to be done; that ſome diſorder might ariſe; that ſome might come to ſave him; and beſides, that it would be a great diſhonour to the Family Royal. Others maintained the contrary, *viz.* That it was abſolutely neceſſary he ſhould paſs through the Town, to
aſtoniſh

of the Empire of MOGOL. 157
aftonifh the World, and to fhew the abfolute Power of *Aureng-Zebe*, and to difabufe the People, that might ftill doubt, whether it were himfelf, as indeed many *Omrahs* did doubt; and to take away all hopes from thofe, who ftill preferved fome affection for him. The Opinion of thefe laft was followed; he was put on an Elephant, his Grand-child, *Sepe-Chekouh*, at his fide; and behind them was placed *Bhadur-Kan*, as an Executioner. This was none of thofe brave Elephants of *Ceilan* or *Pegu*, which he was wont to ride on, with gilt Harnefs and embroidered Covers, and Seats with Canopies very handfomely painted and gilt, to defend themfelves from the Sun: It was an old Caitiff Animal, very dirty and nafty, with an old torn Cover, and a pitiful Seat, all open. There was no more feen about him, that Necklace of big Pearls, which thofe Princes are wont to wear, nor thofe rich Turbants and Vefts embroider'd. All his Drefs was a Veft of courfe Linnen, all dirty, and a Turbant

bant of the same, with a wretched Scarf of *Kachimere* over his head, like a Varlet; his Grand-son, *Sepe-Chekouh*, being in the same equipage. In this miserable posture he was made to enter into the Town, and to pass through the greatest Merchant-streets, to the end that all the People might see him, and entertain no doubt any more whether it was he.

As for me, I fancied we went to see some strange Massacre, and was astonish'd at the boldness of making him thus pass through the Town; and that the more, because I knew that he was very ill guarded, neither was I ignorant, that he was very much beloved by the lower sort of people, who at that time exclaimed highly against the cruelty and tyranny of *Aureng-Zebe*, as one that kept his Father in prison, as also his own Son *Sultan Mahmoud*, and his Brother *Morad-Bakche*. I was well prepar'd for it, and with a good Horse and two good Men I went, together with two others of my Friends, to place

my

my self in the greatest street, where
he was to pass. But not one Man had
the boldness to draw his Sword, only
there were some of the *Fakires*, and with
them some poor 'people, who seeing
that infamous *Gion-Kan* ride by his side,
began to rail and throw stones at him,
and to call him Traitor. All the shops
were ready to break for the crowd of
Spectators, that wept bitterly; and
there was heard nothing but loud Out-
cryes and Lamentations, Invectives,
and Curses, heaped on *Gion-Kan*. In
a word, Men and Women, great and
small (such is the tenderness of the
hearts of the *Indians*) were ready to
melt into tears for compassion; but not
one there was that durst stir to rescue
him. Now after he had thus passed
through the Town, he was put into
a Garden called *Heider-Abad*.

There were not wanting to tell
Aureng-Zebe, how the People at this
sight had lamented *Dara*, and cursed
the *Patan*, that had deliver'd him;
and how the same was in danger to
have been stoned to death, as also that
there

there had been a great apprehenfion of fome fedition and mifchief. Hereupon another Council was held, whether he fhould indeed be carried to *Goualeor*, as had been concluded before; or whether it were not more expedient to put him to death, without more ado? Some were of opinion, that he fhould go to *Goualeor* with a ftrong Guard, that that would be enough; *Danechmend-Kan*, though *Dara*'s old Enemy, infifting much upon that. But *Rauchenara-Begum*, in purfuance of her hátred againft this Brother of hers, pufhed *Aureng-Zebe* to make him away, without running the danger there was in fending him to *Goualeor*; as alfo did all his old Enemies, *Calilullah-Kan*, and *Chah-heft-Kan*, and efpecially a certain Flatterer, a Phyfitian, who was fled out of *Perfia*, firft called *Hakim-Daoud*, and afterwards being become a great *Omrah* named *Takarrub-Kan*: This Villain boldly rofe up in a full Affembly, and cryed out, that it was expedient for the fafety of the State to put him to death immediately, and

of the Empire of MOGOL. 161
and that the rather, becaufe he was no *Muffulman*; that long fince he was turn'd *Kafire*, Idolater, without Religion, and that he would charge the Sin of it upon his own head: Of which imprecation he foon after felt the fmart; for within a fhort time he fell into difgrace, and was treated like an infamous Fellow, and dyed miferably. But *Aureng-Zebe*, carried away by thefe inftances and motives, commanded that he fhould be put to death, and that *Sepe-Chekouh*, his Grandchild, fhould be fent to *Goualeor*.

The Charge of this Tragical Execution was given to a certain Slave, call'd *Nazer*, that had been bred by *Chah-Jehan*, and was known to have been formerly ill treated by *Dara*. This Executioner, accompanied with three or four Parricides more, went to *Dara*, who was then himfelf dreffing fome Lentils with *Sepe-Chekouh* his Grandchild. He no fooner faw *Nazer*, but cryed out to *Sepe-Chekouh*, My dear Son, behold thofe that come to kill us! laying hold at the fame time of
M a fmall

a small Knife, which was all the Arms that were left him. One of these Butchers immediately fell upon *Sepe-Chekouh*; the others, upon the arms and legs of *Dara*, throwing him to the ground, and holding him under, 'till *Nazer* cut his throat. His Head was forthwith carried to the Fortress to *Aureng-Zebe*, who presently commanded it to be put in a dish, and that water should be fetch'd; which when brought, he wiped it off with an Handkerchief, and after he had caused the Face to be washed clean, and the blood done away, and was fully satisfied that it was the very head of *Dara*, he fell a weeping, and said these words; Ah *Bed-bakt*! Ah unfortunate Man! Take it away, and bury it in the Sepulchre of *Houmayon*.

At night, the Daughter of *Dara* was brought into the *Seraglio*, but afterwards sent to *Chah-Jehan*, and *Begum-Saheb*, who asked her of *Aureng-Zebe*. Concerning *Dara*'s Wife, she had ended her days before at *Lahor*: She had poyson'd her self, foreseeing

the

the extremities she was falling into, together with her Husband. *Sepe-Chekouh* was sent to *Goualeor*. And after a few days, *Gion-kan* was sent for, to come before *Aureng-Zebe* in the Assembly: To him were given some Presents, and so he was sent away; but being near his Lands, he was rewarded according to his desert, being killed in a Wood. This barbarous Man not knowing, or not considering, that if Kings do sometimes permit such Actions for their Interest, yet they abhor them, and sooner or later revenge them.

In the mean time, the Governour of *Tatabakar*, by the same Orders that had been required of *Dara*, was obliged to surrender the Fortress. It was indeed upon such a composition as he would have, but it was also with an intention not to keep word with him. For the poor Eunuch, arriving at *Lahor*, was cut in pieces, together with those few Men he had then with him, by *Kalil-ullah-kan*, who was Governour thereof. But the reason of the non-obfervance of the Capitulation was, that there was come intelligence, that he fecretly prepar'd himfelf to go directly to *Soliman-Chekouh*, fparing no Gold, which under-hand he conveyed into the hands of our *Franguis*, and to all thofe that were come with him out of the Fortrefs to follow him, under pretext of accompanying him as far as *Dehli* to *Aureng-Zebe*, who had often faid, that he fhould be very glad to fee fo gallant a Man, and who had fo valiantly defended himfelf.

There remained therefore none of the Family of *Dara*, but *Soliman-Chekouh*, who could not eafily be drawn away from *Serenaguer*, if the *Raja* had been fteady to his firft Declarations. But the fecret practifes of the *Raja Jeffeigne*, the promifes and threats of *Aureng-Zebe*, the death of *Dara*, and the other *Rajas* his Neighbours that had been gain'd, and were prepared by the Orders, and at the coft of *Aureng-Zebe*, to make War againft him, did at laft fhake the Faith of this perfidious

Pro-

of the Empire of MOGOL. 165

Protector, and made him consent to their demands. *Sepe-Chekouh*, who was advertised of it, fled through the midst of those horrid Countries and fearful Desarts, towards the great *Tibet*. But the Son of the *Raja*, soon pursuing and overtaking him, caused him to be assaulted with stones. The poor Prince was hurt, seized, and carried to *Debli*, where he was imprison'd in *Serenguer*, that little Fortress, where at first they had put *Morad-Bakche*.

Aureng-Zebe, to observe what he had practised towards *Dara*, and that no body might doubt it was *Soliman-Chekouh* himself, commanded him to be brought before him in the presence of all the Grandees of the Court. At the entry of the Gate, the Chains were taken from his feet, leaving those he had about his hands, which seemed gilt. When this proper young Man, so handsome and gallant, was seen to enter, there was a good number of *Omrahs* that could not hold their tears; and, as I was informed, all the great Ladies of the Court, that had leave to see him come in, fell a weeping. *Aureng-Zebe*, who appear'd himself to be touched at his misfortunes, began to speak very kindly to him, and to comfort him; telling him amongst other things, that he should fear nothing, that no hurt should be done to him; on the contrary, that he should be well treated, and therefore be of good courage; that he had caused his Father to be put to death for no other reason, than that he was turn'd *Kafer*, and a Man without Religion. Whereupon this young Prince return'd him the *Salem*, and blessed him, abasing his hands to the earth, and lifting them, as well as he could, up to his head, after the custom of the Countrey; and told him with resolution enough, That if he were to drink the *Poust*, he intreated him that he might dye presently, being very willing to submit to his Fate. But *Aureng-Zebe* promised him publickly, that he should drink none of it; that he should rest satisfied as to that, and

not

not entertain any sad thoughts about it. This being said, he once more repeated the *Salem*: And after they had asked him several Questions, in the Name of *Aureng-Zebe*, touching that Elephant which was charged with Roupies of Gold, taken from him when he went to *Serenaguer*, he was sent to *Goualeor* to the rest. This *Poust* is nothing else but Poppy expressed, and infused a night in water. And 'tis that potion, which those that are kept at *Goualeor*, are commonly made to drink; I mean those Princes, whose heads they think not fit to cut off: This is the first thing that is brought them in the morning, and they have nothing given them to eat 'till they have drunk a great cup full of it; they would rather let them starve. This emaciates them exceedingly, and maketh them dye insensibly, they losing little by little their strength and understanding, and growing torpid and senseless. And by this very means 'tis said, that *Sepe-Chekouh*, and the Grandchild of *Morad-Bakche*, and *Soliman-Chekouh*, were dispach'd. As

As to *Morad-Bakche*, he was made away by a more violent death. For *Aureng-Zebe* seeing, that though he was in prison, yet the generality had an inclination to him, and that many Verses were spread in the praise of his Valour and Courage, thought himself not safe enough by putting him to death in private, by giving him *Poust* like others; apprehending, that his Death would be still doubted of, and that that might one time or other occasion some commotion, and therefore devised the following Charge against him.

The Children of a certain *Sayed*, very rich, whom he had caused to be put to death in *Amadevad*, to get his Estate, when he there made his preparations for War, and borrowed or took by force great Sums of Money from all the rich Merchants, appeared in full Assembly, making their complaints, and demanding Justice, and the Head of *Morad-Bakche*, for the Blood of their Father. Not one of the *Omrahs* durst contradict it, both because

of the Empire of MOGOL. 169
cause he was a *Sayed*, that is, one of *Mahomet*'s Kindred, to whom great Veneration was paid; and that every body sufficiently understood the design of *Aureng-Zebe*, taking this for a pretence to rid himself openly of *Morad-Bakche*, under a shew of Justice. So that the Head of him, that had killed the Father of the Plaintiffs, was granted them without any other form of Process. Whereupon they went, with necessary Orders issued out for that purpose, to cut it off in *Goualeor*.

There remained no other Thorn in the Foot of *Aureng-Zebe* but *Sultan Sujah*, who kept himself still in *Bengale*; but he also was forced to yield at last to the power and fortune of *Aureng-Zebe*. There were sent so many Troops of all sorts to *Emir-Jemla*, that at last he was encompassed on all sides, both on this and that side of the River *Ganges*; so that he was necessitated to flye to *Dake*, which is the last Town of *Bengale* on the Sea side; and here comes the conclusion of this whole Tragedy.   This

This Prince being destitute of Ships to put to Sea, and not knowing whither to flye, sent his eldest Son, *Sultan Banque*, to the King of *Racan* or *Moy*, a Heathen or Idolatrous King, to know whether he would give him leave to make his Countrey his place of refuge only for some time, and do him the favour, when the *Mousons* or the Season-winds should come, to furnish him with a Vessel for *Mecha*, from thence to pass into some part of *Turky* or *Persia*. That King sent answer, that he should be very welcome, and have all possible assistance. So *Sultan Banque* returned to *Dake* with some Galeasses, manned with *Franguis* (I mean, with those fugitive *Portugals*, and other straggling Christians, that had put themselves in service to that King, driving no other Trade than to ravage all this lower *Bengale*;) upon which *Sultan Sujah* embarked, with his whole Family, *viz.* his Wife, his three Sons, and Daughters. They were well enough received; whatever was necessary for their
sub-

of the Empire of MOGOL. 171

subsistence, such as that Countrey would afford, was provided for them, in the name of that King. Some months pass, the Season of the favourable Winds come in, but not a word of the Vessel, though he demanded it no otherwise than for his Money; for as yet he wanted not Rupies of Gold, nor Silver, nor Gems: He had too great a plenty of them; his Riches were, in all appearance, the cause of his ruin, or at least contributed much to it. Those barbarous Kings have no true generosity, and are not much refrained by the Faith they have given, regarding nothing but their present Interests, without so much as considering the mischiefs that may befall them for their perfidiousness and brutality. To get out of their hands, one must either be the stronger, or have nothing that may tempt their avarice. *Sultan Sujah* may long enough sollicit for a Vessel; all is in vain, he effects nothing: On the contrary, the King begins to shew much coldness, and to complain of his not
coming

coming to see him. I know not, whether *Sultan Sujah* thought it unworthy of himself, and too mean a thing to give him a Visit; or rather, whether he fear'd, that being in the Kings House he might not there be seized on, to take away all his Treasure, and then be deliver'd into the hands of *Emir-Jemla*, who for that purpose promised, in the name of *Aureng-Zebe*, great Sums of Money, and many other considerable advantages. Whatever the matter was, he would not go thither himself, but sent his Son *Sultan Banque*, who being near the Kings House, began to shew liberality to the people, throwing out to them a good quantity of half Rupies, and whole Rupies, of Gold and Silver. And being come before the King, he presented him with store of Embroideries, and of rare pieces of Goldsmiths-work, set with precious Stones of great value, excusing his Father, *Sultan Sujah*, as being indisposed, and beseeching him in his name, that he would remember the Vessel,

of the Empire of MOGOL. 173
Veffel, and the promife made to him thereof. But all that did not advance his bufinefs; on the contrary, five or fix days after, this King fent to *Sultan Sujah*, to ask of him one of his Daughters in Marriage; which he could never refolve to grant him, whereat this barbarous Prince was highly offended. What then could he do in this cafe? The Seafon paffeth away. What fhall become of him? What other refolution can he take, but to do a defperate Action? Behold a ftrange undertaking, which may give a great Example of what Defpair can do!

Although this King of *Racan* be an Heathen, yet there is in his Dominions ftore of *Mahumetans* mingled with the people, that are retired thither, or have been, for the moft part, taken Slaves, here and there, by thofe *Franguis* above-mention'd. *Sultan Sujah* did under-hand gain thefe *Mahumetans*; and with two or three hundred Men, whom he yet had remaining of thofe that had follow'd him
from

from *Bengale*, he resolved, one day to fall unexpectedly upon the House of this Barbarian, to kill all, and to make himself proclaim'd King of *Racan*. This was a very bold Enterprise, and such a one, as had more of a Desperado in it, than of a prudent Man. Yet notwithstanding, as I was inform'd, and by what I could learn from many *Mahumetans*, and *Portugals*, and *Hollanders*, that then were there present, the thing was feasible enough. But the day before the stroke was to be given, the Design was discover'd; which did altogether overthrow the Affairs of *Sultan Sujah*, and was soon after the cause of his ruin. For not finding hereafter any way more to recover himself, he attempted to flye towards *Pegu*; which was a thing in a manner impossible, by reason of the vast Mountains and Forrests to be passed. Besides, he was immediately pursued so close, that he was overtaken the same day he fled. It may well be thought, that he defended himself with as much courage as was possible.

of the Empire of MOGOL. 175

possible. He killed so many of those Barbarians, that it will scarce be believed, but he was so overpow'red by the multitude of pursuers, that he was obliged to quit the Combat. *Sultan Banque*, who was not so far advanced as his Father, defended himself also like a Lion; but at length, being all bloody of the wounds, by stones poured upon him from all sides, he was seized on, and carried away, with his two little Brothers, his Sisters, and Mother.

As to the Person of *Sultan Sujah* himself, all what could be learnt of it, is this: That he, with one Woman, one Eunuch, and two other persons, got up to the Top of the Mountain; that he received a wound in his Head by a stone, which struck him down, but yet he rose again, the Eunuch having wound his Head about with his Turbant, and that they escaped through the midst of the Woods.

I have heard the Relation three or four other manner of ways, even by those persons that were upon the place.

place. Some did affure, that he had been found among the dead, but was not well known: And I have feen a Letter of the Chief of the *Dutch* Factory, confirming this. So that 'tis difficult enough to know aright what is become of him. And this it is, which hath adminiftred ground to thofe fo frequent Allarms, given us afterwards at *Dehli*: For at one time it was rumored, that he was arrived at *Maflipatan*, to joyn with the Kings of *Golkonda* and *Vifapour*; another time it was related for certain, that he had paffed in fight of *Suratte* with two Ships, bearing the Red Colours, which the King of *Pegu* or the King of *Siam* had given him; by and by, that he was in *Perfia*, and had been feen in *Chiras*, and foon after in *Kandahar*, ready to enter into the Kingdom of *Caboul* it felf. *Aureng-Zebe* one day faid fmiling, that *Sultan Sujah* was at laft become an *Agy* or Pilgrim. And at this very day there are abundance of perfons who maintain, that he is in *Perfia*, returned from *Conftantinople*,

tinople, whence he is said to have brought with him much Money. But that which confirms more than enough, that there is no ground for any of these reports, is that Letter of the *Hollanders*; and that an Eunuch of his, with whom I travelled from *Bengale* to *Maflipatan*, as also the Great Master of his Artillery, whom I saw in the Service of the King of *Golkonda*, have assured me, that he is no more in being, though they made difficulty to say any more concerning him; as also, that our *French* Merchants, that lately came out of *Persia* and from *Hispahan*, when I was yet at *Dehli*, had in those parts heard no news at all of him; besides that, I have heard that a while after his Defeat, his Sword and Poynard had been found: So that 'tis credible, that if he was not killed upon the place, he soon dyed afterwards, and was the prey of some Robbers, or Tygers, or Elephants, of which the Forrests of that Countrey are full. However it be, after this last Action his whole Family was put in Prison, Wives and Children, where they were treated rudely enough; yet some time after they were set at more liberty, and they received a milder entertainment: And then the King called for the eldest Daughter, whom he married.

Whilst this was doing, some Servants of *Sultan Banque*, joyned with divers of those Mahumetans which I have mentioned, went to plot another Conspiracy like the first. But the day appointed for it being come, one of the Conspirators, being half drunk, began too soon to break out. Concerning this also I have heard forty different relations, so that 'tis very hard to know the truth of it. That which is undoubted is this, that the King was at length so exasperated against this unfortunate Family of *Sujah*, that he commanded it should be quite rooted out. Neither did there remain any one of it, that was not put to death, save that Daughter which the King had made his Wife. *Sultan Banque*, and his Brothers, had
their

of the Empire of MOGOL.

their Heads cut off with blunt Axes; and the Women were mured up, where they dyed of hunger and misery.

And thus endeth this War, which the luft of Reigning had kindled among thofe four Brothers, after it had lafted five or fix years, from 1655, or thereabout, to 1660 or 1661; which left *Aureng-Zebe* in the peaceable poffeffion of this puiffant Empire.

The End of the First Tome.

PARTICULAR EVENTS:

OR,

The moſt conſiderable Paſſages after the War, of 5 years, or thereabout,

IN THE

EMPIRE

OF THE

GREAT MOGOL.

Together with a

LETTER

CONCERNING

The Extent of INDOSTAN, the *Circulation* of the Gold and Silver at laſt ſwallow'd up there; the *Riches*, *Forces*, *Juſtice*, and the *Principal Cauſe* of the *Decay* of the STATES of ASIA.

Tom. II.

London, Printed by *William Godbid*, and are to be Sold by *Moſes Pitt*. 1676.

PARTICULAR

EVENTS

IN

THE FIRST

SIEGE

LETTER

PARTICULAR EVENTS:

OR,

The most considerable Passages after the War for Five Years, or thereabout, in the Empire of the GREAT MOGOL.

THe War being ended, the *Tartars* of *Usbec* entertained thoughts of sending Ambassadors to *Aureng-Zebe*. They had seen him fight in their Countrey, when he was yet a young Prince; *Chah-Jehan* having sent him to command the Succours, which the *Kan* of *Samarkand* had desired of him against the *Kan* of *Balk*. They had experienced his Conduct and Valour on many occasions, and they consider'd with themselves, that he could not but remember the Affront they did him, when he was just taking *Balk;* the Capital Town of the Enemy: For the two *Kans* agreed together, and obliged him to retreat, alledging, that they apprehended he might render himself Master of their whole State, just as *Ekbar* had formerly done of the Kingdom of *Kachimere*. Besides, they had certain intelligence of all he had done in *Indostan*, of his Battels, Fortune, and Advantages; whence they might sufficiently estimate, that though *Chah-Jehan* was yet living, yet *Aureng-Zebe* was Master, and the only Person that was to be owned King of the *Indies*. Whether then they feared his just resentments, or whether it was, that their inbred avarice and sordidness made them hope for some considerable Present, the two *Kans* sent to him their Ambassadors to offer him their Service, and to congratulate him upon the happy beginning of his Reign. *Aureng-Zebe* saw very well, that

of the MOGOL. 3

that the War being at an end, this offer was out of seafon, and that it was nothing but fear or hope, as we faid, that had brought them. Yet for all this, he received them honourably, and, fince I was prefent at their Audience, I can relate the particulars of it with certainty.

They made their reverence at a confiderable diftance from him, after the *Indian* cuftom, putting thrice their hands upon their heads, and as often letting them down to the ground. Then they approached fo near, that *Aureng-Zebe* himfelf might very well have taken their Letters immediately from their hands; but yet it was an *Omrah* that took and open'd them, and gave them to him. He forthwith read them with a very grave countenance; and afterwards commanded, there fhould be given to each of them an embroider'd Veft, a Turbant, and a Girdle of Silk in Embroidery, which is that which they call *Ser-apah*, that is, an Habit from head to foot. After this, their Prefents were call'd for, which
con-

consisted in some Boxes of choice *Lapis Lazulus*, divers Camels with long hair, several gallant Horses, some Camel-loads of fresh Fruit, as Apples, Pears, Raisins and Melons; (for 'tis chiefly *Usbec* that furnishes these sorts of Fruit, eaten at *Dehli* all the Winter long;) and in many loads of dry Fruit, as Prunes of *Bokara*, Aprecocks, Raisins without any stones that appeared, and two other sorts of Raisins, black and white, very large and very good.

Aureng-Zebe was not wanting to declare, how much he was satisfied with the Generosity of the *Kans*, and much commended the beauty and rarity of the Fruit, Horses, and Camels; and after he had a little entertain'd them of the state of the Academy of *Samarkand*, and of the Fertility of their Countrey, abounding in so many rare and excellent things, he desired them to go and repose themselves, intimating withall, that he should be very glad to see them often.

They came away from their Audience full of contentment and joy, not being much troubled, that they had been obliged to make their reverence after the *Indian* cuftome, though it have fomething of flavifh in it, nor much refenting it, that the King had not taken their Letters from their own hands. I believe if they had been required to kifs the ground, and even to do fomething of a lower nature, they would have complied with it. 'Tis true, it would have been in vain, if they had defired to make no other falute, but that of their own Countrey, and to deliver to the King their Letters with their own hands; for that belongs only to the Ambaffadors of *Perfia*, nor have thefe this favour granted them, but with much difficulty.

They ftay'd above four months at *Dehli*, what diligence foever they could ufe to be difpatch'd, which did incommode them very much; for they fell almoft all fick, and even fome of them dyed, becaufe they were not accuftomed to fuch heats as are in *Indoftan*, or rather becaufe they were
fordid,

sordid, and kept a very ill Diet. I know not whether there be a more avaricious and uncleanly Nation than they are. They laid up the Money, which the King had appointed them for their maintenance, and lived a very miserable life, altogether unworthy of Ambassadors: Yet they were dismissed with great honour: The King, in the presence of all the *Omrahs*, presented each of them with two rich *Ser-apahs*, and gave order, that eight thousand Rupies should be carried to their Lodgings, which amounted to near two thousand Crowns each. He also gave them, for Presents to the *Kans* their Masters, very handsom *Ser-apahs*, store of the richest and best wrought Embroideries, a good quantity of fine Cloth, and silk Stuffs, wrought with Gold and Silver, and some Tapestries, and two Poynards set about with precious stones.

During their stay, I went thrice to see them, being presented to them as a Physitian by one of my Friends, that was Son of an *Usbec*, that had
made

made his Fortune in that Court. I had a defign to have learned fomething in particular of their Countrey, but I found them fo ignorant, that they knew not fo much as the Confines of their State, much lefs could they inform me of any thing concerning the *Tartars* that have conquer'd *China* of late years: In fhort, they told me nothing that I knew not before. I had once the curiofity to Dine with them, which liberty I obtained eafily enough. They are not Men of much ceremony; it was a very extraordinary Meal for fuch a one as I, it being meer Horfe-flefh; yet for all this I got my Dinner with them; there was a certain Ragou, which I thought paffable: And I was obliged to exprefs a liking of fo exquifit a difh, which they fo much luft after. During Dinner there was a ftrange filence; they were very bufie in carrying in with their whole hands, for they know not what a Spoon is; but after that this Horfe-flefh had wrought in their ftomachs, they began to talk, and then they would

would perfwade me, they were the moft dextrous at Bows and Arrows, and the ftrongeft Men in the World. They call'd for Bows, which are much bigger than thofe of *Indoftan*, and would lay a wager, to pierce an Oxe or my Horfe through and through. Then they proceeded to commend the ftrength and valour of their Women, which they defcribed to me quite otherwife than the *Amazons*; telling me very wonderful ftories of them, efpecially one, which would be admirable indeed, if I could relate it with a *Tartarian* Eloquence, as they did: They told me, that at the time when *Aureng-Zebe* made War in their Countrey, a Party of Twenty five or Thirty *Indian* Horfemen came to fall upon a fmall Village; whilft they plundred, and tyed all thofe whom they met with to make them Slaves, an old Woman faid to them: Children, be not fo mifchievous, my Daughter is not far off, fhe will be here very fhortly, retreat if you be wife, you are undone if fhe light upon you.

of the MOGOL. 9

you. They laughed at the old Woman, and her advice, and continued to load, to tye, and to carry away her self; but they were not gone half a Mile, but this old Woman, looking often backward, made a great out-cry of joy, perceiving her Daughter coming after her on Horse-back; and presently this generous She-*Tartar*, mounted on a furious Horse, her Bow and Arrows hanging at her side, called to them at a distance, that she was yet willing to give them their Lives, if they would carry back to the Village all they had taken, and then withdraw without any noise. The advice of this young Woman affected them as little as that of her old Mother; but they were soon astonish'd, when they found her let fly at them in a moment three or four great Arrows, which struck as many of their Men to the ground, which forced them to fall to their Quivers also. But she kept her self at that distance from them, that none of them could reach her. She laughed at all their effort, and

at

at all their Arrows, knowing how to attack them at the length of her Bow and to take her measure from the strength of her Arm, which was of another temper than theirs: So that after she had killed half of them with her Arrows, and put them into disorder, she came and fell upon the rest with the Zable in her hand, and cut them all in pieces.

The Ambassadors of *Tartary* were not yet gone away from *Dehli*, when *Aureng-Zebe* fell exceeding sick; a violent and continued Fever made him sometimes lose his understanding: His tongue was seized with such a Palsie, that he lost almost his speech, and the Physitians despaired of his recovery; nothing was heard for the time, than that he was gone, and that his Sister *Rauchenara-Begum* concealed his death out of design. It was already bruited, that the *Raja Jessomseigne*, Governour of *Guzaratte*, was on the way to deliver *Chah-Jehan*; that *Mohabet-Kan* (who had at length obeyed the Orders of *Aureng-Zebe*) quitting the Government

of the MOGOL.

ment of *Caboul*, and being already on this side *Lahor* to come back, made haft also with three or four thousand Horse for the same end; and that the Eunuch *Etbar-kan*, who kept *Chah-Jehan* in the Fortress of *Agra*, would have the honour of his delivery. On one side we see *Sultan Mazum* bestir himself exceedingly with bribes, endeavouring by promises to assure himself of the *Omrahs*, so far as that one night he went disguized to the Raja *Jesseigne*, entreating him with expressions of deep respect, that he would engage himself for his interest.

We knew from other hands, that *Rauchenara-Begum*, together with *Teday-kan*, the Great Master of Artillery, and many *Omrahs*, declared for the young Prince *Sultan Ekbar*, the third Son of *Aureng-Zebe*, though he was but seven or eight years old; both parties in the mean time pretending, they had no other design than to deliver *Chah-Jehan:* So that the people believed, that now he was going to be set at liberty, though none of the Grandees

Grandees had any such thing in their thoughts, spreading this rumour only to gain credit and concourse, and because they feared, least by the means of *Etbar-kan*, or some other secret intrigue, he should one day appear in the Field. And indeed of all the parties, there was not one that had reason to wish for his liberty and restoration to the Throne, except *Jessomseigne*, *Mohabet-kan*, and some others, that as yet had done no great matter to his disadvantage. The rest had been all against him, at least they had vilely abandon'd him. They knew very well he would be like an unchain'd Lyon, if he came abroad: Who then could trust him? And what could *Etbar-kan* hope for, who had kept him up so close? I know not, if by some adventure or other, he should have come out of prison, whether he would not have stood single, and been alone of his party.

But though *Aureng-Zebe* was very sick, yet for all this he gave order for all things, and particularly for the

sure

sure cuſtody of *Chah-Jehan* his Father; and though he had adviſed *Sultan Mazum* to go and open the Gates to *Chah-Jehan*, in caſe he ſhould die, yet he omitted not to have *Etbar-kan* inceſſantly writ to. And the fifth day, in the height of his ſickneſs, he cauſed himſelf to be carried into the Aſſembly of the *Omrahs* to ſhew himſelf, and to diſabuſe thoſe who might believe him to be dead, and to obviate popular tumults, or ſuch accident as might have cauſed *Chah-Jehan* to be ſet at liberty. The ſeventh, ninth, and tenth day, he made himſelf to be carried again into the ſaid Aſſembly for the ſame reaſon; and, what is almoſt incredible, the thirteenth, after he had recollected himſelf from a fit of ſwounding, which accaſioned a rumor through the whole Town of his being dead, he called for two or three of the greateſt *Omrahs*, and the Raja *Jeſſeigne*, to let them ſee that he was alive; made himſelf to be raiſed in his bed, called for Ink and Paper to write to *Etbar-kan*, and ſent for the Great Seal, which he had trufted with *Rauchenara-Bagum*, and commonly enclofed in a fmall bag, fealed with a Seal he always wore about his arm, fearing left fhe had already made ufe of it for her defigns. I was nigh my *Agah*, when all this news was told him, and I underftood, that lifting up his hands to Heaven he faid, What a Soul is this? A matchlefs fortitude and courage of fpirit! God preferve thee *Aureng-Zebe*, for greater things; certainly he will not that thou fhouldeft yet die. And indeed after this fit he recover'd by little and little.

He had no fooner recover'd his health, but he fought to get out of the hands of *Chah-Jehan*, and *Begum-Saheb*, the Daughter of *Dara*, to fecure the marriage of *Sultan-Ekbar*, his third Son, with this Princefs; on purpofe thereby to gain him Authority, and to give him the greater right to the Empire; For he it is, who is thought to be by him defigned for it. He is yet very young, but he hath many near and powerful Relations at the Court, and is born of the Daughter of *Chah-Navaze-*

of the MOGOL.

Navaze-kan, and consequently of the Bloud of the Antient Soveraigns of *Machate*; whereas *Sultan Mahmoud* and *Sultan Mazum* are only Sons of *Ragipontnis*, or Daughters of Raja's. These Kings, though Mahumetans, do, for all that, marry of the Daughters of the Heathen, either for State-interest, or for extraordinary Beauty. But *Aureng-Zebe*, was disappointed in this design; It will hardly be believed, with what height and fiercenefs of spirit *Chah-Jehan* and *Begum* rejected the Proposition, and the Young Princefs her felf, who in the fear of being carried away, was for some days desperate, and protested she would rather kill her self an hundred times over, if it were possible, than to marry the Son of him that had murthered her Father.

He had no better satisfaction from *Chah-Jehan* about certain Jewels which he asked of him, in order to finish a piece of work which he caused to be added to a famous Throne, which is so highly esteemed. For he fiercely answer'd, that *Aureng-Zebe* should take no other care but to rule better then he did; that he should let his Throne alone; that he was weary to hear of these Jewels, and that the Hammers were ready to beat them to dust the first time he should be importun'd again about them.

The *Hollanders* would not be the last in doing reverence to *Aureng-Zebe*: they had thoughts of sending an Ambassador to him. They pitched upon Monsieur *Adrican*, the Commander of their Factory at *Suratte*; and being a right honest man, and of good sense and judgment, not neglecting to take the counsel of his friends, he well acquitted himself of this employment. *Aureng-Zebe*, though he carries it very high, and affects to appear a zealous Mahumetan, and consequently to dispise the *Franguis* or Christians, yet thought fit to receive them with much respect and civility. He even was desirous, that this Ambassador should complement him in the mode of the *Franguis*, after he had been made to do it the *Indian* way. 'Tis true, he received

ved his Letters by the hand of an *Omrah*; but *that* was not to be taken for any contempt, he having shew'd no more honour to the Ambassadors of *Usbec*. After this, he intimated to him, that he might produce his Present; and at the same time he caused him, and some of his Train, to be dressed with a *Ser-Apah* embroider'd. The Present cosisted of store of very fine Scarlet, some large Looking-glasses, and divers excellent pieces of Chinese and Japonese work, among which there was a *Paleky*, and a *Tackravan*, or a Field-Throne of admirable workmanship.

This Ambassadour was not so soon dispatch't as he wish'd, it being the custom of the Kings of *Mogol* to detain Ambassodours as long as they well can, from a belief they have, that 'tis the interest of their Greatness, to oblige Strangers to give long attendance at their Court; yet he was not kept so long as the Ambassadours of *Usbec*. Mean time he had the misfortune, that his Secretary died there, and the rest of his Retinue began to grow sick. When the King dismissed him, he gave him such another *Ser-Apah* embroider'd, as the first was for himself; and another, a very rich one, for the General of *Batavia*, together with a Poynard, set about with Jewels, all accompanied with a very obliging Letter.

The chief aim of the *Hollanders* in this Embassy was, to make themselves immediately known to the King, thereby to gain credit, and to intimidate the Governours of the Sea-ports, and other places, where they have their Factories; that so they may not attempt, when they please, to insult over them, or to trouble them in their Trade; thereby letting them know, that they had to do with a potent Nation, and that hath a door open to address themselves, and to complain immediately to the King. Their end also was, to make it appear, what interest the King had in their Commerce; and therefore they shew'd long Rolls of Commodities, bought up by them through the whole Kingdom,

and

and Lifts of confiderable fums of Gold and Silver, every year brought thither by them; but faying not a word of thofe which they draw thence, from the Copper, Lead, Cinamon, Cloves, Mufcadin, Pepper, Wood of Aloes, Elephants, and other Commodities which they vend there.

About this time, one of the moft confiderable *Omrah*'s of *Aureng-Zebe* addreffed himfelf to him, and reprefented, that this multitude and variety of perplexing affairs, and this perpetual attention of mind in him, might foon caufe a great alteration in his temper, and a dangerous inconvenience in his health. But *Aureng-Zebe*, feeming to take almoft no notice of what that *Omrah* faid, turn'd himfelf another way, and approaching to another of the prime *Omrah*'s of the Court, a perfon of great knowledge and judgment, fpoke to him in this purpofe (as I was informed by the Son of this Lord, who was my friend.)

You other Sages, are you not all of the mind, that there are times and conjuncti-
ons

ons so urgent, that a King ought to hazard
his life for his Subjects, and sacrifice himself for their Defence with Arms in his
hands? And yet this Effeminate Man
would disswade me from taking pains, and
dehort me from watching and sollicitude for
the Publick; and carry me by pretences of
Health, to the thoughts of an easie life,
by abandoning the Government of my People, and the management of affairs, to
some Visir or other. Doth he not know,
that Providence having given me a Royal
Extraction, and raised me to the Crown
of Indostan, hath not made me for my
self alone, but for the good and safety of
the Publick, and for the procurement of
tranquility and happiness to my Subjects,
as far as that nay be obtained by Justice and
Power? He seeth not the consequence of
his Counsels, and what mischiefs do attend
Visirships. Doth he think it to be without
reason what out Grand Sady hath so generously pronounced; O Kings, cease, cease
to be Kings, or govern your Kingdoms your
selves? Go tell thy Country-man, that I
shall well like of the care he is constantly to
take of the faithful discharge of his Place;
but

of the MOGOL.

but advise him also, not any more to run out himself so far as he hath done. We have natural *inclination enough to a long, easie, and careless life, and there need no Counsellors to shake off business and trouble. Our Wives, that lye in our bosom, do too often, besides our own genius, incline us that way.*

At the same time there happen'd an accident, that made a great noise at *Dehli*, especially in the Seraglio, and disabused a great many, that could as hardly believe as my self, that Eunuchs, though they had their Genitals quite cut away, could become amorous as other men. *Didar-kan*, one of the chief Eunuchs of the Seraglio, who had built an house, where he came often to divert himself, fell in love with a very beautiful Woman, the Sister of a Neighbour of his, that was an Heathen Scrivener.

These Amours lasted a good while before any body blamed them, since it was but an Eunuch that made them, which sort of men have the priviledge to go where they please; but the

famili-

familiarity grew so great, and so extraordinary betwixt the two Lovers, that the Neighbours began to suspect something, and to rally the Scrivener, which did so touch him, that he threatned both his Sisters and the Eunuch to kill them if they should continue their commerce. And soon after, finding them in the night lying together, he stabbed the Eunuch out-right, and left his Sister for dead. The whole Seraglio, Women and Eunuchs, made a league together against him to make him away; but *Aureng-Zebe* dissipated all these machinations, and was content to have him turn Mahumetan. Mean time 'tis thought, he cannot long avoid the malice and power of the Eunuchs; for 'tis not, as is the common saying, with Men as with Bruits; these latter become gentler and more tractable when they are castrated; but men more vicious, and commonly very insolent, though sometimes it turneth to an admirable fidelity and gallantry.

It was also about the same time, that

Aureng-Zebe was somewhat discontented with *Rauchenara-Begum*, because she was suspected to have given access to two Young Gallants into the Seraglio, who were discover'd and brought before *Aureng-Zebe*. Yet this being but a suspicion, he expressed to her no great resentment of it; nor did he make use of so great rigour and cruelty against those poor men, as *Chah-Jehan* had done against the person above spoken of. The matter was related to me by an old Portuguese Woman (that had a long while been slave to the Seraglio, and went out and in at pleasure) as followeth: She told me that *Rauchenara-Begum*, after she had drawn from a young man, hidden by her, all his abillty, deliver'd him to some Women to convey him away in the night thorough some Gardens, and so to save him: But whether they were discover'd, or whether they feared they should be so, or what else might be the cause, they fled, and left him there wandring in the midst of these Gardens, not knowing which way to get

out

out: And being at laſt met with, and brought before *Aureng-Zebe*, who examined him ſtrictly, but could draw nothing elſe from him, than that he was come in over the walls, he was commanded to get out the ſame way by which he entred: But it ſeems, the Eunuchs did more than *Aureng-Zebe* had given order for, for they caſt him down from the top of the walls to the bottom. As for the other Young Gallant, this ſame Woman aſſured me, that he was found wandring in the Garden like the firſt; and having confeſſed that he was come in by the Gate, *Aureng-Zebe* commanded likewiſe, that he alſo ſhould paſs away again by the ſame Gate; yet reſerving to himſelf a ſevere chaſtiſement for the Eunuchs, ſince not only the honour of the Royal Houſe, but alſo the ſafety of the Kings perſon is herein concerned.

Some months after, there arrived at *Dehli* ſeveral Ambaſſadours, almoſt at the ſame time. The firſt was Xerif of *Meccha*, whoſe Preſent did conſiſt in ſome Arabian Horſes: The ſecond and

and third Ambassador were, he of the King of *Hyeman*, or *Happy Arabia*, and he of the Prince of *Bassora*, who likewise presented Arabian horses. The two remaining Ambassadors were sent from the King of *Ethiopia*. To the three first no great regard was given; they appear'd in so miserable and confused an Equipage, that it was perceived they came only to get some money by the means of their Present, and of the many Horses and other Merchandise, which under the pretence of Ambassadors, entred without paying any duty into the Kingdom, there to be sold, and to buy for the money a quantity of Indian Stuffs, and so to return without paying likewise any Impost at all.

But as to the *Ethiopian* Embassy, that deserves to be otherwise taken notice of; the King of *Ethiopia* having received the news of the Revolution of the *Indies*, had a design to spread his Name in those parts, and there to make known his Grandeur and Magnificence by a splendid Embassy; or, as malice will have

have it, or rather as the very truth is, to reap some advantage by a present as well as the rest. Behold therefore this great Embassy! He chose for his Ambassadors two persons, that one would think were the most considerable in his Court, and the most capable to make such a design prosper. And who were they? the *one* was a Mahumetan Merchant, whom I had seen some years ago at *Moka*, when I passed there coming out of *Egypt* over the *Red-Sea*, where he was to sell some Slaves for that Prince, and to buy of the money, raised thence, some Indian Commodities. And this is the fine Trade of that Great *Christian* King of *Africa*. The *other* was a Christian Merchant of *Armenia*, born and married in *Aleppo*, known in *Ethiopia* by the name of *Murat*. I had seen him also at *Moka*, where he had accomodated me with the half of his Chamber, and assisted me with very good advice, whereof I have spoken in the beginning of this History, as a thing taking me off from passing into *Ethiopia*, according to my first design.

He alſo came every year to that place, in that Kings Name, for the ſame end that the Mahumetan did, and brought the Preſent which the King made every year, to the Gentlemen of the Engliſh and Dutch Company of the *Eaſt-Indies*, and carried away theirs. Now the King of *Ethiopia*, ſutably to his deſign, and the deſire he had of making his Ambaſſadors appear with great ſplendour, put himſelf to great expences for this Embaſſie: He gave them thirty two young Slaves, of both Sexes, to ſell them at *Moka*, and thence to make a ſum of Money to bear their Charges. A wonderful largeſs! Slaves are commonly ſold there for twenty five or thirty Crowns a piece, one with another. A conſiderable ſum. Beſides, he gave them for a Preſent to the *Great Mogol* five and twenty choice Slaves, among which there were nine or ten very young, proper to make Eunuchs of. A very worthy Preſent for a King, and he a Chriſtian, to a Mahumetan Prince! It ſeems the Chriſtianity of the *Ethiopians* is very diffe-

P rent

rent from ours. He added to that Present, twelve Horses, esteem'd as much as those of *Arabia,* and a kind of little Mule, of which I saw the Skin, which was a very great Rarity, there being no Tyger so handsomely speckled, nor Silken Stuff of *India* so finely, so variously, and so orderly streaked, as that was. Moreover, there were for a part of the Present, two Elephants Teeth, so prodigious, that they assured it was all that a very able-bodied man could do to lift up one of them from the ground. Lastly, an Horn of an Oxe full of Civett, and so big, that the aperture of it being measur'd by me, when it came to *Dehli,* it had a Diameter of half a Foot, and somewhat better. All things being thus prepared, the Ambassadors depart from *Gondez,* the Capital of *Ethiopia,* situated in the Province of *Dambea,* and came through a very troublesome Countrey to *Beiloul,* which is a dispeopled Sea-Port over against *Moka,* nigh to *Babel-mandel,* not daring to come (for reasons elsewhere to be

the ordinary way of the
/hich is made with ease in
to *Arkiko*, and thence to
e of *Masoua*. During their
il, and expecting a Bark
waft over the *Red Sea*,
ome of their Slaves, be-
ʒeffel tarried, and they
n that place those refresh-
were necessary for them.
came to *Moka*, they soon
Merchandise to raise a
ɔney according to order.
d this ill luck, that that
ʒes were very cheap; be-
arket was glutted by ma-
:rchants; yet they raised
ɪrsue their Voyage: They
on an Indian Vessel to pass
Their passage was pretty
were not above five and
s at Sea; but whether it
:y had made no good pro-
want of stock, or what
: might be, many of their
Horses, as also the Mule,
ey saved the Skin, died.

They were no sooner arrived at *Suratte*, but a certain Rebel of *Visapour*, called *Seva-Gi*, came and ranscked and burned the Town, and in it their house, so that they could save nothing but their Letters, some Slaves that were sick, or which *Seva-Gi* could not light on, their *Ethiopian* Habits which he cared not for, and the Mules Skin, and the Oxes Horn, which was already emptied of the Civett. They did very much exaggerate their misfortune; but those malicious *Indians* that had seen them arrive in such a wretched condition, without provisions, without habits, without money, or Bills of Exchange, said, that they were very happy, and should reckon the Plunder of *Suratte* for a piece of their best Fortune, forasmuch as *Seva-Gi* had saved them the labour of bringing their miserable Present to *Dehli*, and had furnisht them with a very specious pretence for their beggarly condition, and for the sale they had made of their Civet and of some of their Slaves, and for demanding of

the

the Governour of *Suratte* provisions for their subsistance, as also some Money and Chariots to continue their voyage to *Dehli*. Monsieur *Adrican*, chief of the Dutch Factory, my friend, had given to the Armenian *Murat* a Letter of recommendation to me, which he deliver'd himself at *Dehli*, not remembring that I had been his Host at *Moka*. It was a very pleasant meeting when we came to know one another, after the space of five or six years. I embraced him affectionately, and promised him that I would serve him in whatever I could; but that, though I had acquaintance at the Court, it was impossible for me to do them any considerable good office there: For since they had not brought with them any valuable Present, but only the Mules Skin, and the empty Oxes Horn, and that they were seen going upon the streets without any Paleky or Horses, save that of our Father Missionary, and mine (which they had almost killed) cloathed like Beggars, and followed with seven or eight Slaves, bare-headed ed and bare-foot, having nothing but an ugly Sharſe tyed between their Legs, with a ragged Cloth over their left Shoulder, paſſing under their left Arm like a Summer-Cloak; ſince, I ſaid, they were in ſuch a poſture, whatever I could ſay for them was inſignificant; they were taken for Beggars, and no body took other notice of them. Yet notwithſtanding I ſaid ſo much of the Grandeur of their King to my *Agah Danechmendkan*, who had cauſe to hearken to me, as managing all forreign affairs there, that *Aureng-Zebe* gave them Audience, received their Letters, preſented them each with an embroider'd Veſt, a ſilken embroider'd Girdle, and a Turbant of the ſame, gave order for their entertainment, and diſpatched them in a little time, and that with more honour than there was ground to expect: For in diſmiſſing them, he preſented them each with an other ſuch Veſt, and with 6000 Rupies for them all, which amounteth to about 3000 Crowns, of which the Mahumetan had four thouſand,

of the MOGOL.

sand, and *Murat*, because a Christian, but two thousand. He also gave them for a Present to their Master a very rich *Ser-apah* or Vest, two great silver, and guilt Trumpets, two silver Tymbals, a Poynard cover'd with Jewels, and the value of about twenty thousand Francs in Golden and Silver Rupies, to let their King see Money coyned, as a Rarity he had not in his Countrey: But *Aureng-Zebe* knew very well that these Rupies would not go out of the Kingdom, and that they were like to buy commodities for them: And it fell out so; for they laid them out, partly in fine Cotton Cloth, to make shirts of for their King, Queen, and their only lawful Son that is to be the Successor; partly in silken stuffs streaked with Gold or Silver, to make Vests and Summer-Drawers of; partly in English Scarlet, to make two Arabian Vests of for their King also; and lastly, in Spices, and in store of courier Cloth, for divers Ladies of his Seraglio, and for the children he had by them; all without paying any duty. For

For all my friendship with *Murat*, there were three things that made me almost repent to have served them. The *first*, because *Murat* having promised me to leave with me for 50 Rupies, a little Son of his, that was very pretty, of a delicate Black, and without such a swelled Nose, or such thick Lips as commonly the *Ethiopians* have, broke his word with me, and let me know, that he should take no less for him than 300 Rupies. For all this, I had thoughts of Buying him, for rarities sake, and that I might say, a Father had sold me his Son. The *second*, because I found, that *Murat*, as well as the *Mahumetan*, had obliged themselves to *Aureng-Zebe*, that they would employ their interest with their King, that he might permit in *Ethiopia* to rebuild an old *Mosquee* ruined in the time of the *Portugals*, and which had been Built for a Tomb of a great *Dervich*, which went from *Mecha* into *Ethiopia* for the propagation of *Mahumetanism*, and there made great progress. They received of *Aureng-Zebe* two of the MOGOL. 35

two thoufand Rupies for this engagement. This *Mofquee* had been pulled down by the *Portugals*, when they came with their fuccors into *Ethiopia*, which the then King, who turn'd Catholick, had asked of them againft a *Mahumetan* Prince, Invading his Kingdom. The third, becaufe they defired *Aureng-Zebe*, in the name of their King, to give them an *Alcoran*, and eight other Books, which I well remember, were of the moft reputed in the *Mahumetan* Religion: Which proceeding feemed to me very unworthy of a *Chriftian* Embaffadour, and *Chriftian* King, and confirmed to me what I'had been told at *Moka*, that the *Chriftianity* of *Ethiopia* muft needs be fome odd thing; that it favours much of *Mahumetanifme*, and that the *Mahumetans* increafe exceedingly in that Empire, efpecially fince the *Portugals*, that came in there for the reafon lately expreffed, were either killed, upon the death of the King, by the Cabal of the Queen Mother, or expelled together, with the Patriarch Jefuite,
whom

whom they had brought along from *Goa*.

During the time that the Ambaſſadors were at *Dehli*, my *Agah*, who is more than ordinary curious, made them often come to him, when I was preſent, to inform himſelf of the State and Government of their Country, and principally to learn ſomething of the ſource of the *Nile*, which they call *Ababile*, of which they diſcourſed to us as a thing ſo well known, that no body doubted of it. *Murat* himſelf, and a *Mogol*, who was returned out of *Ethiopia* with him, had been there, and told us very near the ſame particulars with thoſe I had received of it at *Moka*; *viz.* That the *Nile* had its Origine in the Country of *Agaus*; that it iſſued out of the Earth by two Springs bubling up, near to one another, which did form a little Lake of about thirty or forty paces long; that coming out of this Lake, it did make a conſiderable River: and that from ſpace to ſpace it received ſmall Rivers increaſing it.

They

They added, that it went on circling, and making as 'twere a great Iſle; and that afterwards it tumbled down from ſteep Rocks into a great Lake, in which there were divers fruitfuls Iſles, ſtore of Crocodiles, and (which would be remarkable enough, if true) abundance of Sea-calves, that have no other vent for their Excrements than that, by which they take in their food; this Lake being in the Country of *Dambea*, three ſmall daies journey from *Gondar*, and four or five dayes journey from the ſource of the *Nile*: And laſtly, that this River did break out of this Lake, being augmented with many River-waters, and with ſeveral Torrents falling into it, eſpecially in the Rainy Seaſon (which do regularly begin there, as in the *Indies* about *July*, which is very conſiderable and convincing for the inundation of the *Nile*) and ſo runs away through *Sonnar*, the capital City of the King of *Fungi*, Tributary to the King of *Ethiopia*, and from thence paſſeth to the Plains of *Mefre*, which is *Egypt*.

The

The Ambassadors were not wanting to say more than was liked on the subject of their Kings Greatness, and of the strength of his Army; but the *Mogolian* did not over-much agree with them in it; and in their absence represented to us this Army, which he had seen twice in the field, with the *Ethiopian* King on the head of it, as the most wretched thing in the World.

They also related to us divers particulars of that Country, which I have put in my Journal, one day perhaps to be digested and copied: In the mean time I shall insert here three or four things which *Murat* told me, because I esteem them very extravagant for a *Christian* Kingdom. He said then, that there were few men in *Ethiopia*, who besides their lawful Wife, had not many others, and himself owned that he had two, without reckoning her which he had left at *Aleppo*: That the *Ethiopian* Women did not so hide themselves, as they do in the *Indies* among the *Mahumetans*, nor

nor even as among the *Gentils*: That those of the meaner sort of People, Maids or Married Women, Slaves or Free, were often together pell-mell, night and day, in the same Chamber, without those jealousies so common in other Countries: That the Women of Lords did not stick much to go into the House of a simple Cavalier, whom they knew to be a man of Execution: *That* if I had gone into *Ethiopia*, they would soon have obliged me to Marry, as they had done, a few years since, to a certain *European*, who named himself a *Greek* Physician: *That* an ancient man, of about fourscore years of age, did one day present to the King fourscore Sons, all of age, and able to bear Arms; and that the King asked him, Whether he had no more but them? To whom having answer'd, No, but only some Daughters, the King sent him away with this reproach; Begone, thou Calf, and be ashamed for having no more Children at that age, as if Women were wanting in my Dominions!

That

That the King himself had at least fourscore Sons and Daughters running about pell-mell in the Seraglio, for whom he had caused to be made a number of round vernished sticks, made like a little maze; those Children being fond of having that in their hand like a Scepter, distinguishing them from those that were Children of Slaves, or from others living in that place.

Aureng-Zebe sent also twice for these Ambassadors, for the same reason that my *Agah* did, and especially to enquire after the state of *Mahumetanism* in that Country. He had also the curiosity of Viewing the skin of the Mule, which remained, I know not how, in the Fortress amongst the Officers; which was to me a great mortification, because they had designed it for me for the good services I had done them. I made account to have one day presented it to some very curious person in *Europe*. I urged often, that together with the Mules skin, they should carry the great Horn to *Aureng-Zebe*,

shew it him; but they fear'd,
ould make a queſtion, which
ave perplexed them; *viz.*
ame to paſs, that they had
Horn from the plunder of
and loſt the Civet?
theſe Ambaſſadors of *Ethio-*
it *Dehli*, it came to paſs that
ebe called together his Privy
and the moſt learn'd perſons
ourt, to chuſe a new Ma-
his third Son, *Sultan Eck-*
om he deſign'd for his Suc-
In this Councel he ſhew'd the
e hath to have this young
ell Educated, and to make
at Man. *Aureng-Zebe* is not
of what importance it is,
much 'tis to be wiſhed, that
as Kings ſurmount others
neſs, they may alſo exceed
Virtue and Knowledge. He
l knows, that one of the
ſources of the Miſery,
iſ-Goverment, of the un-
, and the decay of the
of *Aſia* proceeds from thence,
that

that the children of the Kings thereof are brought up only by Women and Eunuchs, which often are no other than wrecthed Slaves of *Russia, Circassia, Mingrelia, Gurgistan* and *Ethiopia*; mean and servile, ignorant and insolent souls. These Princes become Kings, when they are of age, without being instructed, and without knowing what 'tis to be a King; amazed when they begin to come abroad out of the Seraglio, as persons coming out of another World, or let out of some subterraneous Cave, where they had lived all their life time; wondring at every thing they meet, like so many Innocents; believing all, and fearing all, like Children, or nothing at all, as if they were stupid: And all this, according to their Nature, and sutable to the first Images imprinted upon them; commonly high and proud, and seemingly grave, but of that kind of pride and gravity, which is so flat and distasteful, and so unbecoming them, that one may plainly see, 'tis nothing but brutality or barbarousness, and

MOGOL. 43

...of some ill-studied and
Documents; or else they
ne childish civilities, yet
oury; or into such cruel-
blind and brutal; or into
nd gross vice of drunken-
) an excessive and altoge-
nable Luxury, either mi-
odies and understandings
Concubines, or altogether
themselves to the pleasures
, like some carniverous A-
ferring a pack of Dogs be-
of to many poor people,
force to follow them in the
heir Game, and suffer to
nger, heat, cold, and mi-
word, they alwayes run
treme or other, being alto-
onal and extravagant. ac-
they are carried by their
xer, or by the first impres-
re given them; thus re-
lmost all, in a strange ig-
what concerns the state of
m; the reins of the Go-
eing abandoned to some
Visir,

Visir; who entertains them in their ignorance and in their passions, which are the two strongest supports he can have to rule alwayes according to his own mind, with most assurance, and the least contradiction; and given over also to those Slaves their Mothers, and to their Eunuchs, who often know nothing but to continue plots of cruelty, whereby they strangle and banish one another, and sometimes the Visirs, and even the Grand Signors themselves; so that no man whatsoever, that hath any Estate, can be in safety of his life.

But to return; after all these Ambassadors, which we have spoken of, there came at last news, that the Ambassador of *Persia* was upon the frontiers. The *Persian* Omrah's, that are at the service of the *Mogol*, spred a rumor that he came for affairs of great importance; though intelligent persons much doubted of a Commission of that nature, considering that the time of great conjunctures was passed; and that those *Omrahs*, and the other *Persi-*
ans

and did what they did, rather to make a show, than for any thing else. Mean time, on the day of the Entry, this Ambassador was received with all possible respect: The *Bazars*, through which he passed, were all new-painted, and the Cavalry attending on the way for above the length of a whole League. Many *Omrah's* accompanied him with Musick, Tymbals and Trumpets, and when he entred into the Fortress, or the Palace of the King, the Guns went off. *Aureng-Zebe* received him with much civility, and was content he should make his Address to him after the *Persian* mode, receiving also, without any scruple, *immediately* from his hands the Letters of his King; which, out of respect, he lifted up even to his head, and afterwards read them with a grave and serious countenance: Which done, he caused an embroider'd Vest to be brought, together with a rich Turbant and Girdle, commanding it to be put on him in his presence. A little after, it was intimated to him, that he might

order

order his Present to be brought in; which consisted of five and twenty as handsome Horses as ever I saw, led, and cover'd with embroider'd trappings; and of twenty very stately and lusty Camels, as big as Elephants: Moreover, of a good number of Boxes, said to be full of most excellent Rosewater; and of a certain distilled water, very precious, and esteemed highly cordial; besides, there were displayed five or six very rich and very large Tapisseries, and some embroider'd pieces exceeding Noble, wrought in small flowers, so fine and delicate, that I know not whether in all *Europe* any such can be met with. To all this were added four Damaskin'd Swords, with as many Poynards, all cover'd with Jewels; as also five or six Harnasses of Horses, which were much esteem'd, being also very fine and rich, the stuff being raised with rich Embroidery set with small Pearls, and very fair Turcoises of the old Rock.

It was observ'd, that *Aureng-Zebe* beheld this Present very attentively; that

that he admired the beanty and rarity of every piece, and that several times he extolled the Generosity of the King of *Persia*; assigning to the Ambassador a place among his chief *Omrahs*. And after he had entertained him a while with a discourse about the inconveniencies and hardships of his Voyage, he dismist him, and made instance, that he should come every day to see him.

During the four or five Months that the Ambassador staid at *Dehli*, he was always splendidly treated at *Aureng-Zebe*'s charge; and the greatest *Omrahs* presented him one after another; and at last he was very honourably dismissed: For *Aureng-Zebe* had him apparell'd with another rich *Serapah* or Vest, to which he added considerable presents for himself, reserving those he intended for his King, 'till he should send an Ambassador expresly; which sometime after he did.

Notwithstanding all these testimonies of honour and respect which *Aureng-Zebe* had shew'd to this Ambassador,

bassador, the same *Persians*, above-spoken of, gave out, that their King had sensibly reproached him in his Letters, with the Death of *Dara*, and the imprisonment of *Chah-Jehan*, as actions unworthy of a Brother, and a Son, and a Musulman; and that he had also hit him with the word *Alem-Guire*, or Conquerour of the World, which *Aureng-Zebe* had caused to be engraven on his Coyn. But 'tis hard to believe, that the King of *Persia* should do any such thing to provoke such a Victorious Prince, since *Persia* is not in a condition to enter into a War with *Indostan*; I am rather apt to believe, that *Persia* hath work enough to keep *Kandahar* on the side of *Indostan*, and the Frontiers on the side of *Turky*: Its Forces and Riches are known; it produceth not always such great Kings as the *Chah-Abbas*, Valiant, Intelligent, and Politick, knowing to make use of every thing, and to do much with small expences. If it were in a condition of undertaking any thing against *Indostan*, or really

sensible

sensible of Piety and the Musal-Man Faith, why was it that in these last troubles and Civil Wars, which continued so long in *Indostan*, the *Persians* sat still and looked on, when *Dara*, *Chan-Jehan*, *Sultan Sujah*, and perhaps the Governour of *Caboul* desired their assistance; and they might with no very great Army, nor great expences have seized on the fairest part of *India*, beginning from the Kingdom of *Caboul*, unto the River *Indus*, and beyond it, and so made themselves Umpires of all things? yet notwithstanding there must needs have been some offensive expressions in those *Persian* Letters, or else the Ambassador must have done or said something that displeased *Aureng-Zebe*; because two or three daies after he had dismissed him, he made a rumour to be spread-abroad, that the Ambassador had caused the Ham-strings of the presented Horses to be Cut; And the Ambassador being yet upon the Frontiers, he made him return all the *Indian* Slaves which he carried along

with

with him, of which he had a prodigious number.

Mean while, *Aureng-Zebe* was not so much concern'd, nor troubled himself so much with this Ambassador, as *Chah-Jehan*, upon a like occasion, did with him, that was sent to him from the Great *Chah-Abbas*. When the *Persians* are in the humor of Rallying against the *Indians*, they relate these three or four little Stories of them: They say, that *Chah-Jehan* seeing that the Courtship and promises made to their Ambassador were not able to prevail with him, so as to make him perform his salute after the *Indian* Mode, he devised this artifice; he commanded to shut the great Gate of the Court of the *Am-kas*, where he was to receive him, and to leave only open the Wicket, through which one man could not pass but very difficultly, by stooping and holding down his Head, as the fashion is when one maketh an *Indian* Reverence, to the end that it might be said, he had made the Ambassador put himself

of the MOGOL.

self in a posture which was something lower than the *Indian* Salam or Salute; but that that Ambassador being aware of this trick, came in with his Back fore-most: And that *Chah-Jehan*, out of indignation to see himself catch'd, told him, *Eh Bed-bakt*, Thou Wretch, dost thou think thou comest into a Stable of Asses, such as thou art? And that the Ambassador, without any alteration, answered; Who would not think so, seeing such a little Door?

Another story is this; That at a certain time *Chah-Jehan* taking ill some course and fierce answers return'd to him by the *Persian* Ambassador, could not hold to tell him; What, hath *Chah-Abbas* no other men at his Court, that he must send to me such a Fool as thy self? And that the Ambassador answer'd; He hath many better and wiser men than me, but *to such a King, such an Ambassador:* They add, that on a certain day *Chah-Jehan*, who had made the Ambassador to Dine in his Presence, and sought some occasion

casion to affront him, seein
was busie in picking and g
Bones, asked him smiling,
Gi, My Lord Ambassador,
the Dogs eat? And that he
readily, *Kichery*, that is,
Pulse, which is the Food of
ner sort of People, and
saw *Chah-Jehan* eat, because
it.

They say also, that c
once asked him, What he t
his new *Dehli* (which he
ding) in comparison of
and that he answer'd aloud,
an oath, *Billah*, *Billah*, *Hi*
not come near the dust of Deh
Chah-Jehan took for a high c
tion, though the Ambassade
him, because the dust is t
some at *Debli*.

Lastly, they relate that c
one day pressing him to tell h
he thought of the Grande
Kings of *Indostan*, compare
of the Kings of *Persia?* He
That, in his opinion, one

better compare the Kings of *India* than to a large Moon of 15 or 16 daies old, and thoſe of *Perſia*, to a ſmall Moon of 2 or 3 dayes. And that this anſwer did at firſt pleaſe *Chah-Jehan*; but that ſoon after he perceived, that that compariſon did him but little honour, the Ambaſſadors ſenſe being, that the Kings of *Indoſtan* were decreaſing, and thoſe of *Perſia* increaſing.

Whether theſe points are ſo commendable, and ſuch marks of wit, every one is free to judge, as he ſeeth cauſe. My opinion is, that a diſcreet and reſpectful gravity is much more becoming Ambaſſadors, than rallery and roughneſs, eſpecially, when they have to do with Kings, who will not be rallied with, witneſs an accident that befell this very Ambaſſador; for *Chah-Jehan* was at length ſo weary of him, and his freedom, that he called him no otherwiſe than Fool; and one day gave ſecret order, that when he ſhould enter into a pretty long and narrow Stree, that is near the Fortreſs, to come to the Hall of the *Aſſembly*, they
ſhould

should let loose upon him an ill-conditioned and fierce Elephant; and certainly, if the Ambassador had not nimbly lept out of his *Paleky*, and, together with his dextrous attendants, shot some Arrows into the Trump of the Elephant, which forced him to turn back he had been utterly spoiled.

It was at this time, upon the departure of the *Persian* Ambassador, that *Aureng-Zebe* received with that admirable wisdome his Tutor *Mallah-sale* the History of which is rare and considerable. This old man, who long since had retired himself towards *Caboul*, and setled himself on some Lands, which *Chah-Jehan* had given him; had no sooner heard of the great fortune of *Aureng-Zebe* his Discipline, who had overcome *Dara* and all his other Brothers, and was now King of *Indostan*, but he came in haft to the Court, swelled with hopes of being presently advanced to no less than the dignity of an *Omrah*. He maketh his Court, and endeavours to engage all his friends, and *Rauchenara-Begum*, the
Kings

of the MOGOL. 55

Kings Sister employs her self for him. But yet there pass three whole Months, that *Aureng-Zebe* does not so much as seem to look upon him; till at length wearied to have him always at his Elbow, and before his Face, he sent for him to a place apart, where there was no body but *Hakim-lul-Mouluk*, *Danech-mend-kan*, and three or four of those *Omrahs*, that pretend to Science, and then spoke to him to this effect (as was informed by my *Agah*.)

What is it you would have of me Doctor? Can you reasonably desire I should make you one of the chief Omrahs *of my Court? Let me tell you, if you had instructed me as you should have done, nothing would be more just: For I am of his perswasion, that a Child well educated and instructed, is as much, at least, obliged to his Master as to his Father: But where are those good Documents you have given me? In the first place you have taught me, that all that* Frangistan *(so it seems they call* Europe *) was nothing, but I know not what little Island, of which the greatest King was he of* Portugal, *and*
next

next to him, he of Holland, and after him he of England; and as to the other Kings, as those of France and Andalusia, you have represented them to me as our petty Raja's; telling me, that the Kings of Indostan were far above them all together, and that they were the true and only Houmajons, the Ekbars, the Jehan-Guyres, the Chah-Jehans, the Fortunate ones, the Great ones, the Conquerors and Kings of the World, and that Persia and Usbec, Kach-guer, Tatar and Catay, Pegu, China, and Matchina did tremble at the name of the Kings of Indostan: Admirable Geography! You should rather have taught me exactly to distinguish all those different States of the World, and well to understand their strength, their way of fighting, their Customs, Religions, Governments & Interests; and by the perusal of solid History, to observe their Rise, Progress, Decay, and whence, how, and by what accidents and errors, those great Changes and Revolutions of Empires and Kingdoms have happened. I have scarce learnt of you the name of my Grandsires, the famous Founders of this

Empire;

Empire; so far were you from having taught me the History of their Life, and what course they took to make such great Conquests. You had a mind to teach me the Arabian Tongue, to read and to write, I am much obliged to you (forsooth) for having made me lose so much time upon a Language, that requires ten or twelve years to attain to its perfection; as if the Son of a King should think it to be an honour to him, to be a Grammarian or some Doctor of the Law, and to learn other Languages than those of his Neighbors, when he cannot well be without them; he, to whom Time is so precious for so many weighty things, which he ought by times to learn. As if there were any spirit that did not with some reluctancy, and even with a kind of debasement, employ it self in so sad and dry an exercise, so longsom and tedious, as is that of learning words.

Thus did *Aureng-Zebe* resent the pedantick Instructions of his Tutor; to which 'tis affirmed in that Court, that after some entertainment which he had with others, he further added the following reproof.

'Know

'Know you not, that Childhood
'well govern'd, being a state which is
'ordinarily accompanied with an hap-
'py memory, is capable of thousand
'of good Preceps and Instructions,
'which remain deeply impressed the
'whole remainder of a mans life, and
'keep the mind alwayes raised for great
'actions? The Law, Prayers, and
'Sciences, may they not as well be
'learned in our Mother-Tongue, as in
'Arabick? You told my Father
'*Chah-Jehan*, that you would teach
'me Philosophy. 'Tis true, I remem-
'ber very well, that you have enter-
'tain'd me for many years with airy
'Questions, of things that afford no
'satisfaction at all to the mind, and
'are of no use in humane society, emp-
'ty Notions, and meer Phancies, that
'have only this in them, that they are
'very hard to understand, and very ea-
'sie to forget, which are only capable
'to tire and spoil a good understand-
'ing, and to breed an Opinion that is
'insupportable. I still remember, that
'after you had thus amused me, I
'know

'know not how long, with your fine
'Philosophy, all I retained of it, was
'a multitude of barbarous and dark
'words, proper to bewilder, perplex,
'and tire out the best wits, and only
'invented the better to cover the va-
'nity and ignorance of men like your
'self, that would make us believe,
'that they know all and that under
'those obscure and ambiguous words,
'are hid great mysteries, which they
'alone are capable to understand: If
'you had seafon'd me with that Philo-
'sophy, which formeth the mind to
'ratiocination, and insensibly accu-
'stoms it to be satisfied with nothing
'but solid reasons; if you had given
'me those excellent precepts and do-
'ctrines, which raise the Soul above
'the assaults of Fortune, and reduce
'her to an unshakeable and always e-
'qual temper, and permit her not to
'be lifted up by prosperity, nor deba-
'sed by adversity; if you had taken
'care to give me the knowledge of
'what we are, and what are the first
'principles of things, and had assisted
'me

'me in forming in my mind a fit Idea
'of the greatnefs of the Univerfe, and
'of the admirable order and motion
'of the parts thereof; if, I fay, you
'had inftilled into me this kind of
'Philofophy, I fhould think my felf
'incomparably more obliged to you
'than *Alexander* was to his *Ariſtotle*;
'and believe it my duty to recompence
'you otherwife, than he did him.
'Should not you, inftead of your
'flattery, have taught me fomewhat
'of that point fo important to a King,
'which is, what the reciprocal duties
'are of a Soveraign to his Subjects,
'and thofe of Subjects, to their Sove-
'raign? And ought not you to have
'confider'd, that one day I fhould be
'obliged with the Sword to difpute
'my Life and the Crown with my Bro-
'thers? Is not that the deftiny almoft
'of all the Sons of *Indoſtan?* Have
'you ever taken any care to make me
'learn, what 'tis to befiege a Town,
'or to fet an Army in array? For thefe
'things I am obliged to others, not at
'all to you. Go, and retire to the Vil-
'lage,

'lage, whence you are come, and let 'no body know who you are, or what 'is become of you.

At that time there arofe a kind of Tempeft againft *Aftrologers*, which did not difpleafe me. Moft people of *Afia* are fo infatuated by *Judiciary Aftrology*, that they believe there is nothing done here below, but 'tis written above (for fo they fpeak.) In all their undertakings therefore they confult Aftrologers. When two Armies are ready to give Battel, they beware of falling on, till the Aftrologer hath taken and determined the moment he fancies propitious for the beginning of the Combat. And fo, when the matter is about electing a Captain-General of an Army, of difpatching an Ambaffador, of concluding a Marriage, of beginning a Voyage, and of doing any other thing, as buying a Slave, putting on new Apparel, &c. nothing of all that is done without the fentence of Mr. Star-Gazer; which is an incredible vexation, and a cuftom drawing after it fuch important confequen-
ces,

ces, that I know not how it can subsist so long. For the Astrologer must needs have knowledge of all that passeth, and of all that is undertaken from the greatest Affairs to the least.

But behold, it happen'd, that the Prime Astrologer of the King was drown'd, which occasioned a great noise at Court, and was a great discredit to Astrology: For he being the person that determined the moments of all enterprizes and actions for the King, and the Omrahs, every one wondred, how a man so experienced, and that for so long time had dispensed good adventures to others, could not foresee his own misfortune. There were not wanting those, who pretended to be wiser than others, and said, that in *Frangistan*, where Sciences did flourish, the Grandees do suspect all such kind of people, and that some hold them even no better than Mountebanks, that 'tis much doubted, whether this Knowledge is grounded upon good and solid
rea-

of the MOGOL.

reasons, and that it may very well be some fancy of Astrologers, or rather an artifice to make themselves necessary to the Great ones, and to make them in some measure to depend on them.

All these discourses very much displeased the Astrologers; but nothing angred them so much as this Story, become very famous, *viz.* That the Great *Chah-Abas* King of *Persia*, commanded to be digged and prepared a little place in his Seraglio to make a Garden; that the young Trees were all ready, and that the Gardner made account to plant them the next day. Mean time the Astrologer taking upon him, said, that a good nick of time was to be observed for planting them, to make them prosper. *Chah-Abas* being content it should be so, the Star-gazer took his Instruments, turned over his Books, made his Calculation, and concluded, that by reason of such and such a Conjunction and Aspect of the Planets, it was necessary they should be set presently. The Master-Gardner, who minded

minded nothing less than this Astrologer, was not then at hand; yet for all that, they fell to work immediately, making holes, and planting the Trees, *Chah-Abas* himself setting them, that it might be said, that they were Trees set with *Chah-Abas*'s own hands. The Gardner returning at night, was sufficiently amazed when he saw the work done; and finding that the right place and order designed by him, was not taken; that, for example, an Apricock-tree stood where an Apple-tree should stand, and a Pear-tree where an Almond-tree; being heartily angry with the Astrologer, caused all the Trees to be plucked up again, and laid them down, with some Earth about them, for next morning, the time chosen by himself. The news hereof came soon to the Ears of the Astrologer, who presently told *Chah-Abas* of it: He forthwith sent for the Gardner, and with some indignation asked him; What had made him so bold as to pull up those Young Trees he had planted with his own hand; that the
time

of the MOGOL. 65

time had been so exactly taken for them, that so good an one would never be had again; and that so he had marred all. The rude Gardner, who had a Cup of *Chiras*-wine in his head, look'd aside upon the Astrologer, and grumbling and swearing, said to him these words, *Billah*, *Billah*, that must needs be an admirable point of time which thou hast taken for these Trees; unhappy Astrologer! They were planted this day Noon and this Evening they have been plucked up again. When *Chah-Abas* heard this, he fell a laughing, turned his back upon the Astrologer, and went away.

I shall here add two particulars, though hapned in the time of *Chah-Jehan*, because such things fall out often enough, and do withal give occasion to observe that ancient and barbarous custom, which makes the Kings of *India* Heirs of the goods of those that die in their service: The first was of *Neiknamkan*, one of the most ancient Omrahs of the Court, and who for the space of 40 or 50 years, wherein

he

had alwayes been employ'd in considerable Offices, had heaped up great store of Gold and Silver. This Lord seeing himself near his end, and thinking upon this unreasonable custom, which often renders the Wife of a great man, upon his decease, poor and miserable in an instant, and necessitates her to present a Petition begging some small pension for her subsistence and for that of her Children, who are constrained to list themselves for common Souldiers under some Omrah; who, I say, considering this with himself, secretly distributed all his Treasure to indigent Knights and poor Widows, filled his Trunks with old pieces of Iron, old shoes, rags and bones, and locked and sealed them, telling every body that they were goods belonging to *Chah-Jehan* the King. These Trunks, after his Death, were brought before *Chah-Jehan*, when he was in the Assembly, and by his command instantly opened in the presence of all the Omrahs, that saw all this fine Stuff, which so provo- and discomposed *Chah-Jehan*, that
he

he rofe in great fury, and went away.

The *other* is only a piece of Gallantry. A rich *Banean*, or Heathen Merchant, being a great Ufurer (as moft of them are) who had alwayes been in employment, and in the pay of the King, came to die. Some years after his death, his Son did extremely importune the Widow, his Mother, to let him have fome Money: She finding him to be a prodigal and debauched Youth, gave him as little as fhe could. This young Fool, by the perfwafion of others like himfelf, made his Complaints to *Chah-jehan*, and was fo filly, as to difcover to him all the goods his Father had left, which amounted to two hundred thoufand Rupies, or hundred thoufand Crowns. *Chah-Jehan*, who foon got an itch for this treafure, fent for the Widow, and commanded her in the open Affembly to fend him an hundred thoufand Rupies, and to give fifty thoufand to her Son, giving order at the fame time to put her away. The old Woman, though
fur-

surprized at this Command, and perplext enough, that she was so suddenly thrust out, without the liberty of speaking, yet lost not her judgment, but with a loud voice gave out, that she had something of moment to discover to his Majesty: Whereupon being brought in again, she said, *God save your Majesty; I find that my Son hath some reason to demand of me the Goods of his Father, as being of his and my flesh and blood, and therefore our Heir; but I would gladly know, what Kindred your Majesty is to my deceased Husband, to be his Heir.* When *Chah-Jehan* heard so plain a piece of rallery, and a discourse of Parentage of the King of the *Indies* with a she-Banian or Idolatrous she-Merchant, he could not hold laughing, and commanded she should be gone, and that nothing should be asked of her.

But to return, I shall not relate all the other considerable things that have happened since the end of the War, that is, since 1660, unto my departure, which was above six years after;
though

of the MOGOL.

though doubtless that would tend much to the design I had in relating the other particulars, which is, to make known the Genius and Temper of the *Mogols* and *Indians*. This I may do in another place: Here I shall only give an account of five or six particulars, which those that shall have read this Relation, will doubtless be curious of.

The *first*, that though *Aureng-Zebe* made *Chah-Jehan* his Father, to be kept in the Fortress of *Agra* with all imaginable care and caution; yet notwithstanding he still left him in his old Apartment with *Begum-Saheb*, his Eldest Daughter, his other Women, Singers, Dancers, Cooks, and others; nothing of that kind was wanting to him. There were also certain *Mullahs*, that were permitted to come and to read the *Alcoran* to him (for he was become very devout.) And when he thought fit, there were brought before him brave Horses, and tamed *Gazelles* (which is a kind of Goat) to make them fight with one another; as also
divers

divers sorts of Birds of prey, and several other rare Animals, to divert him as formerly. *Aureng-Zebe* himself used an art to overcome at last his fierceness and obstinacy, which he had hitherto kept, though a prisoner. And this was the effect of the obliging Letters, full of respect and submission, which he often wrote to his Father, consulting him often as his Oracle, and expressing a thousand cares for him; sending him also uncessantly some pretty Present or other; whereby *Chah-Jehan* was so much gained, that he also wrote very often to *Aureng-Zebe* touching the Government and State-affairs, and of his own accord sent him some of those Jewels, which before he had told him of, that Hammers were ready to beat them to powder the first time he should again ask for them. Besides, he consented that the Daughter of *Dara*, which he had so peremptorily denied, should be deliver'd to him; and granted him at length that pardon and paternal blessing which he had so often desired
with-

without obtaining it. Yet, under all this, *Aureng-Zebe* did not alwayes flatter him; on the contrary, he sometimes return'd sharp anfwers, when he met with ftrains in his Fathers Letters that were pregnant, or expreffed something of his former height and authority. Of this we may judge by the Letter, which I know from a very good hand was once written to him by *Aureng-Zebe*, to this effect:

Sir, You would have me indifpenfably follow thofe ancient Cuftoms, and make my felf Heir to all thofe that are in my pay with the wonted rigour: An Omrah, and even a Merchant can no fooner die, and fometimes even before his death, but we feal up his Trunks, and feize on his goods, and make a ftrict enquiry into his Eftate, imprifoning and ill-treating the Officers of the Houfe to difcover to us all he hath, even to the leaft Jewels. I will believe that there is fome policy in doing fo, but it cannot be denied, that 'tis very rigorous, and fometimes very unjuft; and to fpeak the very truth, we may deferve well enough, that the fame fhould befal us every day,
what

what hapned to you from your Neikman kan, *and from the Widow of your rich Indian Merchant. Moreover* (said he) *it seems, I am by you reputed proud and haughty now I am King: As if you knew not by the experience of more than forty years of your Reign, how heavy an Ornament a Crown is, and how many sad and restless nights it passeth through: as if I could forget that excellent passage of* Mir-Timur (*commonly called* Tamberlan) *which is so seriously delivered to us by that Great Granfather of ours,* Ekbar, *to the end that we might the more weigh the importance and value of it, and consider, whether we have cause to pride our selves so much in a Crown. You well know, that he said, that the same day when* Timur *took* Bajazet, *he made him come before him, and having fixed his eyes on him, fell a laughing; at which* Bajazet *being highly offended, fiercely said to him,* Laugh not at my Fortune; *Timur*; know that 'tis God that is the Dispenser of Kingdoms and Empires; and that the same can befal you to morrow, that hath befallen me to day. *Whereupon*

of the MOGOL.

pon Timur *made this serious and brave Answer;* I know as well as you, *Bajazet,* that 'tis God that distributeth Kingdomes and Empires; I laugh not at your ill Fortune; God forbid I should do so: But beholding your face, I smiled, and had this thought, That certainly these Kingdomes and Empires must in themselves be very little and contemptible things in the eyes of God, since he giveth them to persons so ill made as You and I both are; a deformed one-eyed man, as you; and a lame wretch, as my self. *You require also, that abandoning all my other employments, which I believe very necessary for the establishment and happiness of this State, I should think on nothing but Conquests, and the enlargement of the Empire. I must confess that this is indeed the business of a great Monarch, and of a soul truly Royal, and that I should not deserve to be of the Blood of the Great* Timur, *if I were not of that mind, and had not such inclinations. Mean time, I think I sit not idle, and my Armies are not useless in the Kingdoms of* Decan *and* Ben-

Bengale: *But we must also aver, that the greatest Conquerors are not alwayes the greatest Kings; that we too often see a Barbarian making Conquests, and that those great Bodies of Conquests do ordinarily fall of themselves, and by their own weight. He is a great King, that knows to acquit himself worthily of that Great and August Employment and Charge of Kings, which is to dispence Justice to their Subjects,* &c.

The rest is not come to my hands.

The *second* is in regard of the *Emir-Jemla*. It were to injure this great Man, to pass by with silence his deportment to *Aureng-Zebe* after the War, and the manner of ending his dayes. This eminent person after he had dispatched the Affair of *Bengala* with *Sultan-Sujah* (the second of these four Brothers) not like *Gionkan*, that infamous *Patan* with *Dara*; nor like the *Raja* of *Serenaguer* with *Soliman-Chekouh*; but like a Great Captain and dextrous Polititian, pursuing him as far as the Sea-side, and necessitating him to fly and to escape out of his hands,

hands; after, I say, he had done these things, he sent an Eunuch to *Aureng-Zebe*, intreating him, that he would give him leave to transport his Family to *Bengale*; that now that the War was at an end, and he broken with Age, he hoped he would grant him the advantage of ending his life in the company of his Wife and Children.

But *Aureng-Zebe* is too sharp-sighted, not to pierce into the designs of *Emir*. He seeth him triumphing over *Sujah*; he knows his great credit and reputation, and that he hath the esteem of a very wise, undertaking, valiant and rich man; and that the Kingdom of *Bengale* is not only the best of all *Indostan*, but strong of it self, and further, that this *Emir* is in the head of a well disciplin'd Army, which both honours and fears him. Besides, he is not ignorant of his ambition, and foreseeth well enough, that if he should have with him his Son *Mahmet-Emir-kan*, he would aspire to the Crown, and at least take full possession of *Bengale*, if he should not be able to advance

vance things further. At the same time he is also well aware, that there is danger in refusing him, and that he may possibly prove such a man, as in case of denial, may run into some dangerous extream, as he had done in *Golkonda*. How then, think ye, did he carry himself in this conjuncture? He sends to him his Wife and Daughter, and all the Children of his Son: He maketh the *Emir* a *Mir Ul Omrah*, which is in that Empire the greatest degree of honour that a Favourite can be raised to: And as to *Mahmet-Emirkan*, he maketh him the *Great Bakchis*, which is a dignity and charge like that of our Great Master of the Horse, the second or third Office in the State, but such an one as absolutely obligeth the possessor of it to be alwayes at the Court, not suffering him, but very difficultly, to be absent from the person of the King.

The *Emir* soon perceived, that *Aureng-Zebe* had skilfully put by the stroke, that it would be in vain the second time to ask of him his Son; that he he could not do it without offending him; and that therefore the safest way would be to rest contented with all the testimonies of Friendship, and with all the Honours, together with the Government of *Bengale*; being in the mean time alwayes upon his guard, and in such a posture, that since he could attempt nothing against *Aureng-Zebe*, *Aureng-Zebe* should not be able to attempt any thing against him.

Thus have we seen these two Great Men carry themselves to one another: And in this condition did affairs remain for almost a year; till *Aureng-Zebe*, too well knowing that a great Captain cannot be long at rest, and that, if he be not employed in a Forreign War, he will at length raise a Domestick one; proposed to him to make War upon that rich and potent Raja of *Acham*, whose Territories are on the North of *Dake*, upon the Gulf of *Bengale*. The *Emir*, who in all appearance had already designed this same thing of himself, and who believed, that the Conquest of this Countrey, would

would make way for his Immortal-Honour, and be an occasion of carrying his Arms as far as *China*, declared himself ready for this Enterprize. He embarked at *Dake* with a puissant Army, upon a River which comes from those parts; upon which having gone about an hundred Leagues North-Eastward, he arrived at a Castle called *Azo*, which the Raja of *Acham* had usurped from the Kingdom of *Bengale*, and possessed for many years. He attacked this place, and took it by force in less than fifteen dayes; thence marching over Land towards *Chamdara*, which is the Inlet into the Countrey of that Raja; he entred into it after 26 dayes journey, still Northward: There a Battel was fought, in which the Raja of *Acham* was worsted, and obliged to retreat to *Guerguon*, the *Metropolis* of his Kingdom, four miles distant from *Chamdara*. The *Emir* pursued him so close, that he gave him no time to fortifie himself in *Guerguon*: For he arrived in sight of that Town in five dayes, which constrained the *Raja*, seeing the *Emir's* Army,

of the MOGOL.

Army, to fly towards the Mountains of the Kingdom of *Laſſa*, and to abandon *Guerguon*, which was pillaged, as had been *Chamdara*. They found there vaſt riches, it being a great, very fair and Merchant-like Town, and where the Women are extraordinarily beautiful. Mean time, the ſeaſon of the Rains came in ſooner than uſually; and they being exceſſive in thoſe parts, and overflowing all the Countrey, except ſuch Villages as ſtand on raiſed ground, the *Emir* was much embaraſſed. For the *Raja* made his people of the Mountains come down from all parts thereabout, and to carry away all the proviſions of the Field; whereby the *Emir*'s Army (as rich as 'twas) before the end of the rains fell into great ſtreights, without being able to go forward or backward. It could not advance, by reaſon of the Mountains very difficult to paſs, and continually peſter'd with great Rains; nor retreat, becauſe of the like Rains and deep wayes; the *Raja* alſo having cauſed the way to be digged up as far as to *Chamdara*: So that the *Emir* was forced to remain in that wretched condition during the whole time of the Rain; after which, when he found his Army diftafted, tired out, and half ftarved, he was neceffitated to give over the Defign he had of advancing, and to return the fame way he was come. But this Retreat was made with fo much pains, and fo great inconveniencies, by reafon of the dirt, the want of victuals, and the purfuit of the *Raja* falling on the Rear, that every body (but he) that had not known how to remedy the diforder of fuch a March, nor had the patience to be fometimes five or fix hours at one paffage to make the Souldiery get over it without confufion, would have utterly perifh'd, himfelf, Army, and all; yet he, notwithftanding all thefe difficulties and obftacles, made a fhift to come back with great honour and vaft riches. He defign'd to return thither again the next year, and to purfue his undertaking, fuppofing that *Azo*, which he had fortified, and where he left a ftrong Gar-

Garrison, would be able to hold out the rest of the year against the *Raja*. But he was no sooner arrived there, but Fluxes began to rage in his Army: Neither had himself a body of Steel more than the rest; he fell sick and died, whereby Fortune ended the just apprehensions of *Aureng-Zebe*. I say, the *Just* apprehensions; for there was none of those that knew this great man, and the state of the affairs of *Indostan*, who did not say, 'Tis this day that *Aureng-Zebe* is King of *Bengale*. And himself could not forbear to express some such thing; for he publickly said to *Mahmet-Emir-kan*; You have lost your Father, and I the greatest and the most dangerous Friend I had; yet notwithstanding he comforted this Son, and withal assured him, that he would ever be a Father to him. And whereas 'twas thought, that he would at least cut off his Salary, and make Inquisition into his Treasury, he confirmed him in his Office of *Bakehis*, augmented his Pension to a thousand Rupies a moneth,

and

and left him Heir of all the Estate of his Father, although the Custom of the Country empowred him to seize on all.

The *third* is concerning *Chah-hest-kan*, whom *Aureng-Zebe* made first Governour of *Agra*, when he went out to the Battel of *Kaajoue* against *Sultan Sujah*; and afterward, Governour and General of the Army in *Decan*; and at last, after the death of *Emir-Jemla*, Governour and General of the Army in *Bengale*, together with the charge of *Mirul Omrah* which *Emir-Jemla* had possessed. This *Chah-hest-kan* is he, whom in our History we have mention'd as Uncle to *Aureng-Zebe*, and one that hath so much contributed to his happiness by his eloquent and skilful pen, as well as by his intrigues and counsels. It would be injurious to his Renown also, to be silent of the important enterprise, which he undertook presently when he entred upon his Government; and that the rather, because *Emir-emla*, whether out of policy, or for another cause,

of the MOGOL. 83

cause, had no mind to tempt him; as also, because the particularities, which I am going to relate, will shew not only the passed and present state of the Kingdoms of *Bengale* and *Rakan*, which hitherto hath not been well described to us by any; but also some other things that are worth knowing.

To the end therefore that the importance of *Chah-hest-kan*'s attempt may be well understood, and a good Idea be had of what passeth about the Gulf of *Bengale*, we are to know, that these many years there have always been in the Kingdom of *Rakan* or *Moy*, some *Portuguese*, and with them a great number of their *Christian* Slaves, and other *Franguis*, gather'd from all parts. That was the refuge of the Run-aways from *Goa*, *Ceilan*, *Cochin*, *Malague*, and all those other places, which the *Portugueses* formerly held in the *Indies*; and they were such as had abandoned their Monasteries, men that had been twice or thrice Married, Murtherers: In a word,
such

such as had deserved the Rope, were most welcome and most esteem'd there, leading in that Country a life that was very detestable, and altogether unworthy of Christians, insomuch that they impunely butchered and poysoned one another, and assassinated their own Priests, who sometimes were not better than themselves. The King of *Rakan* in the apprehension he hath ever had of the *Mogol*, kept them for a guard of his Frontiers, in a Port-Town called *Chategon*, giving them Land, and liberty to live as they pleased. Their ordinary Trade was Robbery and Piracy. With some small and light Gallies they did nothing but coast about that Sea, and entring into all Rivers thereabout, and into the Channels and Arms of *Ganges*, and between all those Isles of the lower *Bengale*, and often penetrating even so far as forty or fifty leagues up into the Countrey, surprized and carried away whole Towns, Assemblies, Markets, Feasts and Weddings of the poor Gentiles, and others of that Countrey, making Women Slaves, great and small, with strange cruelty; and burning all they could not carry away. And thence it is, that at present there are seen in the mouth of *Ganges* so many fine Isles quite deserted, which were formerly well peopled, and where no other Inhabitants are found but wild Beasts, and especially Tygers.

This great number of Slaves, which thus they took from all quarters, behold what use they made of. They had boldness and impudence enough, to come and sell to that very Country the old people, which they knew not what to do with; where it so fell out, that those who had escaped the danger by flight, and by hiding themselves in the Woods, labour'd to redeem to day their Fathers and Mothers, that had been taken yesterday. The rest they kept for their service, to make Rowers of them; and such Christians as they were themselves, bringing them up to robbing and killing; or else they sold them to the *Portugneses* of *Goa, Ceilan, St. Thomas*, and others; and even

to

to those that were remaining in *Bengale* at *Ogouli*, who were come thither to settle themselves there by the favour of *Jehan-Guyre*, the Grandfather of *Aureng-Zebe*, who suffered them there upon the account of Traffick, and of his having no aversion to Christians, as also because they promised him to keep the Bay of *Bengale* clear from all Pyrats. And it was towards the Isle of *Galles*, near the Cape of *Palmes*, where this fine Trade was. These Pyrates lay there in wait at the passage for the *Portugueses*, who filled their Ships with them at a very easie rate; this infamous Rabble impudently bragging, that they made more Christians in one year, then all the Missionaries of the *Indies* in ten; which would be a strange way of enlarging Christianity.

These were the Pyrates that made *Chah-Jehan*, who was a more zealous Mahumetan than his Father *Jehan-Guyre*, to express at last his passion, not only against the Reverend Fathers the *Jesuites*, Missionaries of *Agra*, in that of the MOGOL. · 87

that he caufed to be pulled down the beft part of a very fair and large Church that had been built, as well as that of *Lahor*, by the favour of *Jehan-Guyre*, who, as I faid, did not hate Chriftianity; and upon which there ftood a great Steeple with a great Bell in it, whofe found might be heard over all the Town; not only, I fay, againft thofe *Jefuites*, but alfo againft the Chriftians of *Ogouli*: For being impatient to fee them connive at the Pyrates, to make the name of the *Franguis* formidable, and to fill their houfes with Slaves that were his own Subjects, he wafted and utterly ruined them, after he had both with fair words and menaces drawn from them as much money as he could: And becaufe they were indifcreetly obftinate, in refufing what he demanded of them, he befieged them, and caufed them all to be brought to *Agra*, even their very Children, their Priefts and Friers. This was a mifery and a defolation not to be parallell'd; a kind of *Babilonian* tranfmigration. There they were all
made

made Slaves: The handsom Women were shut up in the Seraglio; the old Women and others, were distributed among divers *Omrahs*. The young Lads were circumcised, and made Pages; and men of age renounced for the most part their Faith, either terrified by the threatnings they heard daily, that they should be trampled upon by Elephants, or drawn away by fair Promises. 'Tis true, that there were some of those Friers, who persisted, and that the Missionaries of *Agra*, who notwithstanding all this unhappiness, remained in their houses, found means afterwards, partly by Friends, partly by Money, to get many of them away, and to have them conveyed to *Goa*, and to other places belonging to the *Portugueses*.

They were also the same Pyrates, who some time before the desolation of *Ogouli*, offered to the Vice-Roy of *Goa* to put the whole Kingdom of *Rakan* into their hands for the King of *Portugal*; but he refused, they say, this offer, out of arrogance and jealousie;
and

would not send the succours, which for that end was demanded of him by a certain *Bastian Consalve*, who had made himself head of those people, and was become so potent and considerable, that he married one of the Kings Daughters; being unwilling that it should be said, that a man of so mean Extraction as this *Bastian* was, had done such a Master-piece. But it may be said on this occasion, that this is not much to be wondred at, considering that the *Portuguese* in the *Indies* by such a conduct have divers times been faulty on the like occasions, in *Japan*, in *Pegu*, in *Ethiopia*, and other places; not to mention, that by this way, and that perhaps by a just Divine chastisement (as they all frankly confess themselves) they are become a prey to their Enemies, and fallen so low in the *Indies*, that I know not whether they will ever recover more; whereas formerly, before they were corrupted by vice, and degenerated through pleasure, they made all others tremble in those parts; forasmuch

much as then they were brave and generous men, zealous for the Chriſtian Religion, conſiderable for gallant exploits and for riches; all the *Indian* Kings ſeeking their friendſhip.

Beſides this, the ſame Pyrates ſeized at that time on the Iſle of *.ondiva*, an advantageous Poſt to command a part of the Mouth of *Ganges*: In which Iſle a certain *Auguſtin* Frier, a very famous man, acted the King for many years, having taken a courſe, God knows how, to rid himſelf of the Commander of that place.

Moreover, the ſame Robbers took *Sultan-Sujah* at *Daka*, to carry him away in their Galeaſſes to *Rakan*, as we related above, and found means to open his Coffers, and to rob him of good ſtore of Jewels, which afterwards were ſecretly, and at a very cheap rate, ſold in *Rakan*, moſt of them being fallen into the hands of people that had no skill in them, and afterwards into the hands of the *Hollanders*, and others, who knew how to buy them up quickly, making thoſe

fellows

fellows believe, that they were soft Diamonds, and that they would pay them according to the *degrees* of their hardnefs.

Laftly, They are they that for many years have given exercife to the Great *Mogol* in *Bengale*; having obliged him here to keep alwayes Garrifons every where upon the Paffes, and a great Militia, and a Fleet alfo of Galeaffes to oppofe their courfes, and who, notwithftanding all this, have made fhift to make ftrange devaftations, and ofen to enter far into the Country, and to laugh at all the Souldiery of the *Mogols*; in regard they were become fo bold, and fo dextrous at their Weapons, and fo skilful in piloting their Galeaffes, that four or five of them tuck not to fet upon fourteen or fifteen *Mogolians*, which they alfo actually worfted, and took, or run aground. And upon thefe Pyrates *Chah-heft-kan* caft his eyes as foon as he came into *Bengale*, taking a refolution to deliver the Countrey of this plague of people, that had fo long wafted it; and defign-

T ing

ing afterwards to pafs on, and to attack the King of *Rakan*, according to the order of *Aureng-Zebe*, who at any price had a mind to revenge the blood of *Sultan-Sujah*, and all his Family, that had been fo cruelly handled, and to teach that Barbarian, how the Blood Royal was to be regarded and efteemed on any occafion whatfoever, Behold now with what dexterity *Chahheft-kan* carrieth on his defign!

Knowing that 'tis impoffible to pafs any Cavalry by Land, no not fo much as any Infantry, from *Bengale* into *Rakan*, becaufe of the many channels and rivers upon the Frontiers; and alfo that on the other fide, thofe Pyrates of *Chatigon*, whom we juft now were fpeaking of, would be powerful enough to hinder him from tranfporting them by Sea; he thought upon this experiment, *viz.* to engage the *Hollanders* in his defign. He therefore fent a kind of Ambaffador to *Batavia*, empowering him to treat upon certain Conditions, with the General of that Company, joyntly to fubdue

due the whole Kingdom of *Rakan*; as formerly *Chah-Abbas* subdued that of *Ormus*, in conjunction wirh the *English*. The General of *Batavia* seeing the thing to be possible, and that it was a means more and more to break the *Portugneses* in the *Indies*, and that it would turn to a very good account to the Company, dispatcht away two Men of War for *Bengale*, to favour the transportation of the *Mogolian* Troops in spight of those Pyrates. But observe what *Chah-hest-kan* did before these Men of War arrived: He equipped a great number of Galeasses, and many large Vessels to transport the Army; threatned the Pyrates, utterly to spoil and ruine them; acquainted them with the design of *Aureng-Zebe* upon *Rakan*; that a potent Army of the *Dutch* was near; that they should think on themselves and their families, if they were wise; and in a word, if they would abandon the service of the King of *Rakan* and take that of *Aureng-Zebe*, he would procure very good conditions for them, distribute amongst them as much Land in *Bengale* as they desired, and pay them the double of what they had now.

'Tis doubtful, whether these Menaces and Promises made impression upon them, or whether it was not an accident that moved them; they having about that time assassinated one of the chief Officers of the King of *Rakan*, and apprehending a punishment for that crime: However it be, they were caught, and they were one day struck with such a panick terror, that they shipp'd themselves all at once in forty or fifty of their Galeasses, and wasted over to *Bengale* to *Chah-hest-kan*, and that with so much precipitation, that they hardly took time to embark their Wives and Children, and what else was most precious to them. *Chah-hest-kan* received them with open arms, courted them exceedingly, gave them very considerable pay, and without letting them cool, made them, joyntly with his whole Army, to attack and take the Isle of *Sondiva*, which was fallen into the hands of the King of *Ra-*

Rakan; and thence to pass with all his Horse and Foot to *Chatigon*. About this time the two *Holland*-Vessels arrived; but *Chah-hest-kan*, who thought that henceforth it would be easie for him to compass his design, thanked them. I saw these Ships in *Bengale*, and their Commanders, who were but little contented with such thanks and liberalities of *Chah-hest-kan*. As to the Pyrates, since now he holds them fast, and hopeless of ever returning to *Chatigon*, and hath no more need of them, he makes nothing of all those large promises he made them, and treats them not as he should, but as they deserve, leaving them whole moneths without pay, and not looking upon them otherwise than Traitors and infamous men, unfit to be trusted, after they have so vilely deserted him, whose Salt they had eaten so many years. After this manner did *Chah-hest-kan* put an end to this Rabble, which, as I said, have ruined and dispoiled all the lower *Bengale*. Time will shew whether he will be as happy in the remainder of his Enterprize againſt the King of *Rakan*.

The *fourth* particular is concerning the two Sons of *Aureng-Zebe*, viz. *Sultan Mahmoud*, and *Sultan Mazum*. He ſtill keeps the firſt of them in *Goualeor*, but (if one may believe the common report) without making him take the *Pouſt*, which is the ordinary Drink of thoſe that are put into that place. As to the *other*, though he hath alwayes been a pattern of reſervedneſs and moderation, yet one knows not whether he was not too forward in making a party, when his Father was ſo extreamly ſick; or whether *Aureng-Zebe* have not upon other occaſions perceived ſomething that might give him cauſe of jealouſie; or whether he had not a mind to make an authentick proof of both his Obedience and Courage. However it be, one day he commanded him in an unconcerned manner, in a full Aſſembly of the *Omrahs*, to go and kill a *Lyon*, that was come down the Mountains, and had made great havock and

and waste in the Countrey; and this he did without giving order to furnish him with those strong and large Nets, which they are wont to employ in this dangerous kind of hunting in a real mood; telling the great Hunting-Master, who presently called for those Nets, that when he was Prince, he did not look for such Formalities. It was the good fortune of *Sultan Mazum*, that he prosper'd in this attempt, not losing any more than two or three men, and some horses that were wounded, although, on the other hand, the matter went not off so pleasantly, the wounded *Lyon* having leapt up to the head of the Sultan's Elephant. Since that time, *Aureng-Zebe* hath not been backward to express much affection to him;· he hath given him even the Government of *Decan*, though with so little power and treasure, that there is no great cause to apprehend any thing upon that account.

 The *fifth* thing toucheth *Mohabet-kan*, the Governour of *Kabul*, whom

Aureng-Zebe took from his Government, and generously pardoned; not willing, as he said, to lose so brave a Captain, and that had stuck so close to his Benefactor *Chah-Jehan*. He made him even Governour of *Guzuratte*, in the place of *Jessemseignue*, whom he sent to make War in *Decan*. It may very well be, that some considerable Presents he made to *Rauchenara-Begum*, and a good number of excellent *Persian* Horse and Camels, wherewith he presented *Aureng-Zebe*, together with fifteen or sixteen thousand Rupies of Gold, did contribute to make his peace.

On this occasion of mentioning the Government of *Kaboul*, which borders upon the Kingdom of *Kandahar*, which is now in the hands of the *Persians*, I shall here briefly add some particulars, that serve to this History, and will still more discover that Country, and declare the Interests between *Indostan* and *Persia*, which no body, that I know of, hath explained hitherto.

Kan-

of the MOGOL. 99

Kandahar, that strong and important place, which is the Capital and the swaying City of this Noble and Rich Kingdom of the same Name, hath in these latter Ages been the subject of grievous Wars between the *Mogols* and *Persians*, each of them pretending a right thereto. *Ekbar*, that great King of the *Indies*, took it by force from the *Persians*, and kept it during his life. And *Chah-Abbas*, that famous King of *Persia*, retook it from *Jean-Guyre*, the Son of *Ekbar*. Afterwards it return'd to *Chah-Jehan*, Son of *John Guyre*, not by the Sword, but by the means of the Governour *Aly-Merdan-kan*, who surrendred it to him, and went over to live at his Court, apprehending the Artifices of his Enemies, who had brought him into disfavour with the King of *Persia*, that sent for him to make him give an accompt, and to deliver up his Government. The same City was beseiged and retaken afterwards by the Son of *Chah-Abbas*, and since that besieged twice again, yet without being

ing taken, by *Chah-Jehan*. The first time it was saved from being taken by the ill understanding and jealousie between the *Persian* Omrahs, that are Pensioners of the *Great Mogol*, and the most powerful of his Court, as also by the respect they bear to their Natural King: For they all behaved themselves very effeminately in the Siege, and would not follow the *Raja Roup*, who had already planted his Standards upon the Wall on the side of the Mountain. The second time it was saved by the jealousie of *Aureng-Zebe*, who would not fall into the breach of the Wall, that our *Franguis*, the *English*, *Portugueses*, *Germans*, and *French* had made by their Canon, though it was a large one; being unwilling to have it said, that in the time of *Dara*, who was in a manner the first mover of that Enterprise, and was then in the City of *Caboul*, with his Father *Chah-Jehan*, the Fortress of *Kandahar* was taken. *Chah-Jehan*, some years before the late trouble, was also ready to besiege it the third time, had not

Emir-

of the MOGOL.

Emir-Jemla diverted him from it, advising him to turn his Forces towards *Decan*, (as hath been said;) with whom *Aly-Merdan-kan* himself concurred, who was so earnest in his disswading him from it, as to say to him these words, which I shall punctually relate, as having something extravagant in them:

Your Majesty will never take Kandahar, *unless you had such a Traytor there as my self; except you were resolved never to bring a* Persian *into it, and to make the Bazars or Markets wholly free, that is, to lay no Impost on those that furnish the Army with provision.*

At length, *Aureng-Zebe*, like the others, had prepared himself in these latter years to besiege it also; whether it was that he was offended at the tart Letters, written to him by the King of *Persia*, or by reason of the affronts and ill treatment which he had offered to *Tarbiet-kan* his Ambassador; that hearing of the King of *Persia*'s death, he turned back, saying, (which yet is not very credible) that he he would not meddle with a Child, a new King; although *Chah-Soliman*, who hath succeeded his Father, is, in my opinion, about 25 years of age.

The *sixth* particular we purposed to speak of, concerns those that have faithfully served *Aureng-Zebe*. Those he hath almost all raised to great places. For first, as we have already related, he made *Chah-hest-kan*, his Uncle, Governour and General of the Army of *Decan*, and afterwards, Governour of *Bengale*. Next, he made *Mir-kan* Governour of *Kaboul*; Then *Kalilullah-kan*, of *Lahor*; and *Mirhaba*, of *Elubas*; and *Lasker-kan*, of *Patna*. The Son of that *Allah-Verdi-kan* of *Sultan Sujah*, he appointed Governour of *Scimdy*; and *Fazel-kan*, who had considerably served him both by his counsels and dexterity, he made *Kane-saman*, that is, Great Steward of the House Royal: And *Danechmend-kan*, Governour of *Dehli*, with this particular grace and priviledge, that since he is perpetually employed in studies and forreign affairs,

he

he so dispenseth with him for not coming twice a day (after the ancient custom) to wait on the King in the Assembly, as not to retrench any thing of his pension for his absence, as he doth to the other Omrahs, if they fail. He hath given to *Dianet-kan* the Government of *Kachmire* (aliàs *Caffimere*) that little, and in a manner inaccessible Kingdom, which *Ekbar* seized on by craft, that Earthly Paradise of the *Indies*; which hath its Histories written in its peculiar Language; whereof I have an abridgement in the *Persian* Tongue, made by the command of *Jehan Guyre*, containing a large Catalogue of many very ancient Kings, that often were so powerful, that they subdued the *Indies* as far as *China*.

'Tis true, that *Aureng-Zebe* dismissed *Nejabat-kan*, who did very well in the two Battels of *Samonguer* and *Kadjoue*, but then 'tis not fit at all, that a Subject should ever reproach his King, as he did, with the services done him.

As

As to those infamous men, *Gion-kan* and *Nazer*, 'tis known, that the former hath been recompenced as he deserved; but the other no man knows what is become of him.

What concerns *Jessomseigne* and *Jesseigne*, there is something as to them that is intricate, which I shall endeavour to unfold. There is a certain Heathen revolted from the King of *Visapour*; who knew how to possess himself of many important Fortresses, and of some Sea-ports of that King. His name is *Seva-Gi*, that is, Lord *Seva*. He is a stout man, vigilant, bold, and undertaking in the highest degree, who gave *Chah-hest-kan* more work and trouble in *Decan*, than the King of *Visapour* with all his forces, and all his *Raja*'s joyned with him for their common defence: Insomuch that having designed to take away *Chah-hest-kan* and his Treasures out of the midst of his Army and of the Town *Aurenge-Abad*, he carried on his design so far, that he had effected it, if he had not been discovered a little too

of the MOGOL.

too foon ; for one night, accompanied with a number of refolute Fellows he hath about him, he was got into the very apartment of *Chah-heft-kan*, where his Son, who was forward in the defence, was killed, and himfelf grievoufly wounded ; *Seva-Gi* in the mean time getting away as well as he came: Who for all this was fo far from being daunted, that he undertook another very bold and very dangerous enterprife, which fucceeded much better. He took two or three Thoufand chofen men of his Army, with whom he took the Field without noife, fpreading a report by the way, that it was a *Raja* going to the Court. When he was near *Suratte*, that Famous and Rich Port of the *Indies*, inftead of Marching further (as he made the Great Provoft of that Country, whom he met, believe) he fell into that Town, where he ftaid about three Dayes, cutting off the Arms and Legs of the Inhabitants, to make them confefs where were the treafures;

fearcing,

searching, digging, and loading away, or burning what he could not carry with him. Which done, he returned, none opposing his return, loaden with millions of Gold, Silver, Pearls, Silken Stuffs, Fine Linnen, and other rich Merchandise. *Jessomseigne* was suspected ,to have had since intelligence with this *Seva-Gi*, which was the cause that *Aureng-Zebe* called him away from *Decan* ; but he, instead of going to *Dehli*, went to his own Territory.

I forgot to mention, that in the plunder of *Suratte*, that Ring-leader *Seva-Gi*, like a Saint, had so much respect to the House of the Reverend Father *Ambrose* , a Missionary *Capucian*, that he gave order it should not be plundered; because, said he, I know that the Fathers *Franguis* are good men. He had also regard to the House of the Deceased *De Lale* , because he understood that he had been Great Almoner. He also consider'd the Houses of the *English* and *Dutch*, not from Devotino, as he did the former, but because

they

they were in a good posture of defence; especially the *English*, who having had time to send for assistance from some of their ships that lay near the Town, behaved themselves gallantly, and saved, besides their own, several other houses near them. But a certain *Jew* of *Constantinople*, who had brought Rubies of a very great value, to sell them to *Aureng-Zebe*, carried away the Bell from all, by saving himself from the hands of *Seva-Gi*; for, rather than to confess that he had any Jewels, he was brought thrice upon his knees, and the knife held up to cut his throat: But it became none save a *Jew*, hardned in avarice, to escape in such a manner.

Touching *Jesseigne*, King *Aureng-Zebe* made him content to go General of the Army in *Decan*, sending *Sultan-Mazum* with him, without any power. He presently and vigorously besieged the principal Fortress of *Seva-Gi*, and knowing more than all the rest in matter of Negotiation and Treaty, he so ordered the business, that *Seva-Gi* surrendred

rendred before it came to extremity; and then he drew him to *Aureng-Zebe*'s party againſt *Viſapour*, King *Aureng-Zebe* declaring him a *Raja*, taking him under his protection, and giving the penſion of a very conſiderable *Omrah* to his Son. Some time after, *Aureng-Zebe* deſigning to make War againſt *Perſia*, wrote to *Seva-Gi* ſuch obliging Letters touching his Generoſity, Ability and Conduct, that he made him reſolve, upon the faith of *Jeſſeigne*, to come to him to *Dehli*. There a kinſwoman of *Aureng-Zebe*, the Wife of *Chah-heſt-kan* (who was then at Court) by the influence ſhe had upon the ſpirit of *Aureng-Zebe*, perſwaded him to arreſt him that had murdered her Son, wounded her Husband, and ſacked *Suratte*: So that one evening *Seva-Gi* ſaw his Pavilions beſet with three or four *Omrahs*; but he made ſhift to get away in the night. This eſcape made a great noiſe at Court, every one accuſing the Eldeſt Son of the Raja *Jeſſeigne* to have aſſiſted him in it. *Jeſſeigne*, who preſently had news that

Au-

Aureng-Zebe was very angry with him and his Son, and was advised no more to go to the Court, was day and night upon his guard, apprehending left *Aureng-Zebe* should take this for a pretence to fall upon his Lands, and possess himself of them. Whereupon he also soon left *Decan* to secure his Estate; but when he was at *Brampour*, he died. Yet notwithstanding *Aureng-Zebe* was so far from expressing any coldness or resentment to the Son of *Jesseigne*, that he sent to condole with him for the Death of his Father, and continued to him his Pension; which confirms what many say, that it was by the consent of *Aureng-Zebe* himself, that *Seva-Gi* escaped, forasmuch as he could retain him no longer at Court, because all the Women there had too great a spleen against him, and looked upon him as a man that had embroiled his hands in the blood of his Kinsmen.

But to return to *Decan*, we are to consider, that that is a Kingdom, which these forty years hath constantly been the Theater of War, and upon the

V 2 score

score whereof the *Mogol* hath much to do with the Kings of *Golkonda*, and of *Vifapour*, and divers little Soveraigns; which is not to be underſtood, unleſs it be known, what conſiderable things have paſſed in thoſe parts, and the condition of the Princes that govern them.

All this great Peninſule of *Indoſtan*, cutting it from the Bay of *Cambaja* unto that of *Bengale*, near *Jaganrate*, and paſſing thence to Cape *Comori*, was ſcarce two hundred years ſince entirely (ſome mountanous parts excepted) under the Dominion of one only Prince, who conſequently was a very great and very potent Monarch: But now it is divided among many different Soveraigns, that are alſo of different Religions. The cauſe of this diviſion was, that the King *Ramras*, the laſt of thoſe that have poſſeſſed this mighty State entirely, did imprudently raiſe three Slaves, *Gurgis*, he had about him too high, ſo as to make them all three Governors of places: The *firſt*, of the greateſt part of thoſe Countries, which at

pre-

present are possessed by the *Mogol* in *Decan*, about *Daulet-Abad*, from *Bider*, *Parenda*, *Sarette*, unto *Narbadar*: The second, of all the other Lands, now comprehended under the Kingdom of *Visapour*: And the *third*, of all that is contained under the Kingdom of *Golkonda*. These three Slaves grew very rich, and found themselves supported by a good number of the *Mogols*, that were in the service of *Ramras*, because they were all three Mahumetans, of the Sect *Chyas*, like the *Persians*. And at length they all revolted together with one accord, killed King *Ramras*, and returned to their Government, each taking upon him the Title of *Chah* or King. The Issue of *Ramras*, not finding themselves strong enough for them, were content to keep themselves in a Corner, *viz.* in that Countrey which is commonly called *Karnatek*, in our Maps *Bisnagar*, where they are still *Raja*'s to this very day. All the rest of the State was also at the same time divided into all those *Rajas Naiques* and petty Kings, such as we see there.

These

These three Slaves and their posterity have alwayes defended themselves very well in their Kingdoms, whilst they kept a good mutual correspondence, and assisted one another in their grievous wars against the *Mogols*. But when they once came to think every one to defend their Lands apart, they soon found the effects of their division. For the *Mogol* so well knew to take his time upon that occasion (which is now about thirty five or forty years since) that he possessed himself within a little time of all the Countrey of *Nejam-Chah*, or King *Nejam*, the fifth or sixth of the family of the first Slave, and at last took him prisoner in *Daulet-Abad*, the Capital, where he died.

After that time, the Kings of *Golkonda* have maintained themselves well enough; not as if they could compare with the power of the *Mogol*, but because the *Mogol* hath alwayes been employed against the two others; from whom he was to take *Amber*, *Paranda*, *Bider*, and some other places, before he could conveniently march towards

Gol-

of the MOGOL.

Golkonda. And becaufe they have always been fo politick, being very opulent, as to furnifh under hand the King of *Vifapour* with Money, and thereby to help him to maintain a War againft the *Mogol*: Befides that, they ever have a confiderable Army on foot, which is alwayes ready, and never fails to take the Field, and to approach to the Frontiers, at the time when there is news that that of the *Mogol* marches againft *Vifapour*; to let the *Mogol* fee, not only that they are alwayes ready to defend themfelves, but alfo that they could eafily affift the King of *Vifapour*, in cafe he fhould be reduced to any extremity. Next, which is very confiderable, they know alfo how to convey Money under hand to the Chieftains of the *Mogolian* Army; who thereupon advife the Court, that it is more to purpofe to attack *Vifapour*, as being nearer to *Daulet-Abad*. Further, they fend every year very confiderable Prefents to the Great *Mogol*, by way of Tribute; which confift partly in fome rare manunufactures of the Countrey; partly in Elephants, which they send for from *Pegu*, *Siam*, and *Ceilan*, partly in fair ready money. Lastly, the *Mogol* considers that Kingdom as his own, not only because he looks upon the King thereof as his Tributary, but chiefly since that agrement heretofore spoken of, which the present King made with *Aureng-Zebe*, when he besieged *Golkonda*; and there being also no place able to resist, even from *Daulet-Abad* unto *Golkonda*, he judgeth, that when he shall think fit to push for it, he may take in the whole Kingdom in one Campagne; which in my opinion, he would certainly have done, if he did not apprehend, lest sending his Forces towards *Golkonda*, the King of *Visapour* should enter into *Decan*; as, no doubt, he would do, knowing it to be very important to his conservation, that that Kingdom may alwayes subsist as now it is.

From all which, something may be understood of the Interests and Government of the King of *Golkonda*

with

with the *Mogol*, and what way he taketh to support himself against him. Yet notwithstanding all this, I find this state much shaken, in regard that the King that now is, since that unhappy affair of *Aureng-Zebe* and *Emir-Jemla*, seems to have lost heart, and as 'twere abandoned the reins of the Kingdom, not daring any more to go forth of this Fortress of *Golkonda*, nor so much as appear in publick to give Audience to his People, and to render Justice according to the custom of the Country: Which discomposeth things very much, and occasions the Grandees to tyrannize over the meaner sort of People, and to lose even their respect to the King, often slighting his Commands, and considering him no more than a Woman; and the People, weary of the injustice and ill treatment, breathing after nothing but *Aureng-Zebe*. 'Tis easie to judge of the streights this poor King is in, by four or five particulars I am about to relate.

The first, that *An.* 1667. when I was
at

at *Golkonda*, King *Aureng-Zebe* having sent an Ambassador Extraordinary to declare War to that King, unless he would furnish him with 10000 Horse against *Visapour*, he did extraordinary honour, and give excessive presents to that Ambassador, as well for him in particular, as for *Aureng-Zebe*, and made an agreement with him, to send him; not 10000 Horse, but as much Money as is necessary to maintain so many; which was all that *Aureng-Zebe* looked for.

The second is, that *Aureng-Zebe*'s Ambassador in Ordinary, that is constantly at *Golkonda*, commands, threatens, striketh, gives Pass-ports, and saith and doth whatsoever he will, no man daring with the least word to cross him.

The third is, that *Mahmet-Emir-kan*, the Son of *Emir-Jemla*, though he be no more than a simple Omrah of *Aureng-Zebe*, is yet so much respected through that whole Kingdom, and especially in *Maslipatan*, that the *Taptata*, his Commissioner,

of the MOGOL.

oner, is as 'twere Master thereof, buying and selling, bringing in and sending abroad his Merchants Ships, no body daring to contradict him in any thing, nor to demand any Customs. So great was once the power of *Emir-Jemla* his Father in this Kingdom, which time hath not yet been able to root out.

The fourth is, that the *Hollanders* scruple not to threaten him sometimes, to lay an Embargo upon all the Merchants Ships of the Country that are in that Port, and not to let them go out, untill their demands be granted; as also to put in protestations against him: which I have seen actually done, upon the account of an *English* Vessel, which they had a mind to take by force in the Port of *Maslipatan* it self, the Governour having hindred it, by arming the whole Town against them, and threatning to put fire to their Factory, and to put them all to death.

A fifth is, that the *Portuguese*, as poor, and miserable, and decayed as
they

they are in the *Indies*, yet ſtick not to threaten that King alſo with War and that they will come and ſacſ *Maſlipatan*, and all that Coaſt, if h will not render them that place of St *Thomas*, which ſome years ago they choſe to put into his hands, rather thai to be conſtrained to yield it up to th *Dutch*.

Yet for all this, I have been inform ed in *Golkonda*, by very intelligent per ſons, that this King is a Prince of ver great judgment, and that whatever h ſo does and ſuffers, is only in policy to the end to provoke no body, anc principally to remove all ſuſpitior from *Aureng-Zebe*, and to give him to underſtand, that he hath in a manner no ſhare any more in the Kingdom But that in the mean time a Son of his that is kept hid, grows up, the Father watching for a fit time to declare hin King, and ſo to laugh at the agreement made with *Aureng-Zebe*. Of this time will ſhew us more; in the mean time, let us conſider ſomewhat of the Intereſts of *Viſapour*.

The

The Kingdom of *Visapour* hath also not been wanting to support it self, though the *Mogol* do almost continually make war against it; not so much as if he of *Visapour* were able to bid head to the *Mogolian* Forces, but because there is never any great effort used against him. For it is not very frequent there, no more than 'tis elsewhere, for Generals of Armies to desire the end of a War; there being nothing so charming, as to be in the head of an Army, commanding like little Kings, remote from the Court. It is also grown to a Proverb, that *Dean* is the Bread and Life of the Souldiers of *Indostan*. Besides, the Counrey of *Visapour* is on the side of the *Mogol*'s Dominions of a very difficult access, upon the account of the scarcity of good Waters, Forrage, and Victuals; and because *Visapour*, the Capital City, is very strong, and situate in a dry and steril Countrey, there being almost no good Water but in the Town. And lastly, because there are many Fortresses in that Countrey,

trey, seated on Hills hard to climb

Yet notwithstanding all this, tha State is much shaken, if considering that the *Mogol* hath taken *Paranda*, the Key, as 'twere, of that Kingdom; a also that fair and strong Town *Bider* and some other very important places But principally because the last King of *Visapour* died without Heirs Males and he that now calls himself King, is a Youth, whom the Queen, Sister of the King of *Golkonda*, hath raised, and taken for her Son (a favour for which he hath made an ill return, having shew'd no esteem for this Queen after her return from *Mecca*, under the pretext of some ill demeanour in her of a *Dutch* Vessel that carried her to *Moka*:) Lastly, because that in the disorders of that Kingdom, the Heather Rebel, *Seva-Gi*, above discoursed of found means to seize on many strong Holds, mostly seated on steep Mountains, where he now acteth the King laughing at the *Visapour* and the *Mogol* and ravaging the Countrey every where, from *Suratte* even to the gate

o

of *Goa*. This notwithstanding, if he wrongs *Visapour* one way, he helps to support it another, forasmuch as he is resolutely bent against the *Mogol*, preparing alwayes some Ambush, and cutting so much work for his Army, that there is no discourse, no apprehension but of *Seva-Gi*; insomuch that he hath come and sacked *Suratte*, and pillaged the Isle of *Burdes*, which belongs to the *Portuguese*, and is near the Gates of *Goa*.

The *seventh* particular, which I learn'd at *Golkonda*, when I was come way from *Dehli*, is the death of *Chah-ehan*; and that *Aureng-Zebe* had been xceedingly affected therewith, having iscover'd all the marks of grief, that a on can express for the loss of his Father: That at the very hour of receiing that news, he went towards *A-ra*; that *Begum-Saheb* caused the Mosuee, and a certain place, where he as at first to stop, before he entred e Fortress, to be hung with richly nbroider'd Tapisseries: That at his tring into the Seraglio, she presented

him

him with a great Golden Bason, wherein were all her Jewels, and all those of *Chah-Jehan*; and in short, that she knew to receive him with so much Magnificence, and to entertain him with that dexterity and craft, that she obtained his pardon, gain'd his favour and grew very confident with him.

To conclude, I doubt not, but most of those, who shall have read my History, will judge the wayes taken by *Aureng-Zebe*, for getting the Empire very violent and horrid. I pretend no at all to plead for him, but desire only that before he be altogether condemned, reflexion be made on that unhappy custom of this State, which leaving the succession of the Crown undecided, for want of good Laws, setling it, as amongst us, upon the eldest Son, exposeth it to the Conquest of the strongest, and the most fortunate, subjecting at the same time all the Princes born in the Royal Family, by the condition of their Birth, to the cruel necessity either to overcome, or to reign by destroying all the rest, for the assurance

rance of their power and life, or to perish themselves, for the security of that of others: For I am apt to believe, that upon this confideration the Reader wil not find *Aureng-Zebe*'s conduct so strange as at first it appear'd. However I am perswaded, that those who shall a little weigh this whole History, will not take *Aureng-Zebe* for a Barbarian, but for a great and rare Genius, a great States-man, and a Great King.

A Letter to the Lord COLBERT, *of the Extent of* Indoſtan; *the Circulation of Gold and Silver, coming at length to be ſwallowed up, there, as in an Abyſs; the Riches, Forces, Juſtice, and the principal Cauſe of the decay of the States of* Aſia.

My Lord,

SInce it is the cuſtom of *Aſia*, never to approach Great Perſons with empty hands, when I had the honour to kiſs the Veſt of the Great *Mogol Aureng-Zebe*, I preſented him with eight

eight *Roupies* * as an ex- *A Roupy is about
preſſion of reſpect; and half a Crown,
the illuſtrious *Fazel-kan*, the prime
Miniſter of State, and he that was to
eſtabliſh my Penſion as Phyſitian, with
a Caſe of Knives garniſhed with Amber. *My Lord*, though I intend not
to introduce new cuſtoms in *France*,
yet I cannot forget this upon my return
from thoſe parts; being perſwaded,
that I ought not to appear before the
King, for whom I have a far deeper veneration than for *Aureng-Zebe*, nor before *You*, *My Lord*, for whom I have a
much higher eſteem than for *Fazel-kan*, without ſome little Preſent to
both, which is rare, at leaſt for its novelty, though it be not ſo upon the
account of the preſenting hand. The
Revolution of *Indoſtan* by reaſon of its
extraordinary occurrences and events,
hath to me ſeemed worthy of the
Greatneſs of our Monarch, and this
Diſcourſe, for the quality of the matters therein contained, ſutable *to* the
rank you hold in his Counſels; *to*
that Conduct, which at my return

appeared to me so admirable in the Order, which I found setled in so many things, that I thought incapable of it; and *to* the passion you entertain to make it known to the ends of the Earth, what a Monarch we have, and that the *French* are fit to undertake, and with honour to atchieve, whatsoever you shall have designed for their honour and advantage.

'Tis in the *Indies*, *My Lord* (whence I am lately return'd after twelve years absence) where I learn'd the felicity of *France*, and how much this Kingdom is obliged to your cares; and where your Name is so diffused, and so well known. This were a fair Theme for me to enlarge upon; but my Design being no other than to discourse of things *New*, I must forbear to speak of those that are already so notorious to all the world. I shall doubtless please you better, by endeavouring to give you some *Idea* of the state of the *Indies*, which I

I have engaged my felf to give you an account of.

My Lord, you may have feen before this, by the Maps of *Afia*, how great every way is the extent of the Empire of the Great *Mogol*, which is commonly call'd *India* or *Indoftan*. I have not meafur'd it Mathematically; but to fpeak of it according to the ordinary journeys of the Country, after the rate of three whole Months March, traverfing from the Frontiers of the Kingdom of *Golkonda*, as far as beyond *Kazni* near *Kandahar*, which is the firft Town of *Perfia*, I cannot perfwade my felf otherwife, but that it is at leaft five times as far as from *Paris* to *Lyons*, that is, about five hundred common Leagues.

Next, you may pleafe to take notice, that of that vaft extent of Land, there are large Countries that are very fertil, and fome of them to that degree (for example, that whole great Kingdom of *Bengale*) that they exceed thofe of *Egypt*, not only upon the account of the abundance of Rice, Corn, and all other things neceſſary for life, but alſo upon the ſcore of all thoſe Commodities ſo confiderable, which *Egypt* is deſtitute of, as Silks, Cottons, Indigo, and ſo many others, ſufficiently related by Authors.

Moreover, that of theſe ſame Countries there are many that are well enough peopled and cultivated, and where Trades-men, though naturally very lazy there, are not wanting, either from neceſſity or other Cauſes, to apply themſelves to work, as to Tapiſſeries, Embroideries, Cloth of Gold and Silver, and to all thoſe kinds of Silk and Cotton Manufactures, that are uſed in the Countrey, or tranſported to other parts.

You may further obſerve, how that Gold and Silver circulating as it were upon the Earth, comes at laſt in part to be ſwallowed up in this *Indoſtan*. For of that which comes out

out of *America*, and is difperfed through the feveral Kingdoms of our *Europe*, we know, that one part is carried into *Turky* many wayes, for the Commodities drawn thence; and that another part is conveyed into *Perfia*, by the way of *Smyrna*, for the Silks afforded there : That all *Turky* generally needs *Coffee*, which comes out of *Hyeman* or *Happy Arabia*, and is the common Drink of the *Turks*: That the fame *Turky* as well as *Hyeman* and *Perfia* cannot be without the Commodities of *India*; and that thus all thofe Countries are obliged to carry to *Moka* over the Red-Sea, near *Babelmandel*; and to *Baffora* the utmoft part of the *Perfian-Gulf*; and to *Bandar-Abbafi*, or *Gomoron* near to *Ormus*, a part of that Gold and Silver, that had been brought into their Country, to be thence tranfported into *Indoftan*, in Veffels, that yearly, in the feafon of the *Mounfons*, come purpofely to thofe those three famous parts: That on the other hand, all those Ships of *India*, whether they be *Indian* ones, or *Dutch*, or *English*, or *Portuguese*, that every year Transport Merchandise out of *Indostan* to *Pegu*, *Tanasseri*, *Siam*, *Ceilan*, *Achem*, *Macasser*, the *Maldives*, *Mosambic*, and other places, bring back also much Gold and Silver from all those Countries, which meets with the same Destiny, that the other doth: That of that quantity of Gold and Silver which the *Hollanders* draw from *Japan* (which is stored with Mines) a part also comes to be at length discharged in this *Indostan*; And that lastly what is carried thither directly by Sea, whether from *Portugal*, *England*, or *France*, seldom comes back from thence but in Merchandise, the rest remaining there, as the former.

I very well know, that it may be said, that this *Indostan* needs Copper, Cloves, Nutmegs, Cinamon, Elephants, and sundry other things, which

which the *Hollanders* carry thither from *Japan*, the *Molucques*, *Ceilan*, and *Europe*; as alſo that it hath occaſion for Lead, which in part, it is furniſh'd with out of *England*; likewiſe for Scarlet, which it hath from *France*; Moreover, that it ſtands in need of a good number of Horſes, it being certain, that from the ſide of *Usbec* it receives yearly more than 2500. That out of *Perſia* alſo it is furniſhed with abundance of the ſame; as alſo out of *Ethiopia*, *Arabia*, the Ports of *Moka*, *Baſſora*, and *Bander-abbaſy*: Beſides that it needs that ſtore of freſh Fruit, which comes thither from *Samarkand*, *Ball-bocara*, and *Perſia*, as Melons, Apples, Pears, and Grapes, that are ſpent at *Dehli*, and bought at great Rates, almoſt all the Winter long; as well as dry Fruit, which are had there all the year long, and come from the ſame Countries, as Almonds, Piſtaches, Nuts, Prunes, Abricots, Raiſins, and the like: And that laſtly,

lastly, it wants those little sea-cockles of the *Maldives*, which serve for common Coyn in *Bengale*, and in some other places; as also Ambergriece, carried thither from the said *Maldives* and *Mosambic*, Rhinoceros-horns, Elephants-teeth, Musk, China-dishes, Pearls of *Baharen*, and *Tutucoury* near *Ceilan*; and, I know not of how many other things of this kind.

But all this makes not the Gold and Silver to go out of that Empire, because the Merchants at their return freight their ships with the Commodities of the Country, finding a better account by so doing, than if they should bring back Money, so that that hinders not, but that *Indostan* proves, as we have said, a kind of abyss for a great part of the Gold and Silver of the World, which finds many ways to enter there, and almost none to issue thence.

In a word, you may take notice, that this *Great Mogol* makes himself heir of the *Omrahs* or Lords, and of the

the *Manfeb-dars*, or petty Lords, that are in his Pay; and (which is of very great confequence) that all the Lands of that Empire are his propriety, excepting fome Houfes and Gardens; which he giveth leave to his Subjects to fell, divide, or buy amongft them, as they fhall think fit.

Thefe are the things, which fufficiently fhow, *both* that there muft needs be a very great ftore of Gold and Silver in *Indoftan*, though there be no Mines; *and* alfo that the *Great Mogol*, the Soveraign of the fame, at leaft, of the beft part of it, hath immenfe Revenues and Riches.

But on the other hand, there are alfo many things to be obferved, which are a poife to thefe Riches. The *firft*, that among thofe vaft tracts of Land there is much, which is nothing but fand and fterill Mountains, little Tilled or Peopled: That even of thofe that would be fertile, there is much, that is not ufed for want of Workmen, fome of which have perifh'd by the too evil treatment of the Governours, who

who often take from them their necessary lively-hood, and sometimes their
very Children whom they make slave
when they are not able, or are unwilling to pay: Others have abandoned
the Field for the same reason, and de-
sponding out of the consideration that
they labour'd only for others, have cast
themselves into Towns or into Armies
to serve there for Porters, or waiting
men, and many have fled to the lands
of the *Rajas*, because there they found
less tyranny, and more kindness.

The *second* is, That in this same
extent of Country there are sundry
Nations, which the *Mogol* is not full
Master of, most of them retaining
yet their particular Sovereigns and
Lords, that obey him not, nor pay
him tribute but from constraint; many, that do little; some that do nothing at all; and some also, that receive tribute from him, as we shal
see anon. Such are those petty Sovereigns, that are seated on the Frontiers of *Persia*, who almost never pay
him any thing, no more than they do

the MOGOL. 155
of *Perſia*: As alſo the *Ba-*
Augans, and other Moun-
f whom alſo the greateſt
n but a ſmall matter, and
but very little for him :
affront they did him, when
his whole Army by cut-
Water, which they kept
the Mountains, when he
Atek on the River *Indus* to
ly ſiege to *Kandahar*; not
Water to run down into
where was the High-way,
ad received preſents, al-
7 asked them by way of
:h are alſo the *Patans*; a
People, iſſued from the
iver *Ganges* towards *Ben-*
iefore the Invaſion of the
lia, had taken their time
emſelves potent in many
chiefly at *Dehli*, and to
y *Rajas* thereabout their
Theſe *Patans* are fierce
, and even the meaneſt
hough they be waiting
rters, are ſtill of a very
high

high spirit, being often heard to say by way of swearing; *Let me never be King of* Dehli, *if it be not so*: A People that despise the *Indians*, *Heathen*, and *Mogols*, and mortally hate the last, still remembring what they were formerly, before they were by them driven away from their large Principalities, and constrained to retire hither and thither, far from *Dehli*, and *Agra*, into the Mountains, where now they are setled, and where some of them have made themselves petty Sovereigns, like *Rajas*, but of small strength.

Such an one also is the King of *Visapour*, who pays to the *Mogol* nothing, and is always in War with him; maintaining himself in his Country, partly by his own forces, partly because he is very remote from *Agra* and *Dehli*, the ordinary places of Residence of the Great *Mogol*; partly also because his Capital City *Visapour* is strong and of difficult access to an Army, by reason of the ill Waters and the want of Forrage on the way; and

of the MOGOL.

and partly becaufe many *Rajas* joyn with him for their common defence, as did the famous *Seva-gi*, who not long fince came pillaging and burning that rich Sea-port, *Suratte*, and who fometimes will pay little or no Tribute.

Such is likwife that potent and rich King of *Golkonda*, who under-hand gives Money to the King of *Vifapour*, and hath always an Army ready on the Frontiers for his own defence, and for the affiftance of *Vifapour*, in cafe he find him too much preffed.

Of the like fort are more than an hundred *Rajas*, or confiderable Heathen Sovereigns, difperfed through the whole Empire, fome near to, others remote from *Agra* and *Dehli*: amongft whom there are about fifteen or fixteen that are very rich and puiffant; fuch as is *Rana* (who formerly was, as 'twere, Emperour of the *Rajas*; and who is faid to be of the Progeny of King *Porus*;) *Jeffeigna* and *effom feigna*, which are fo great and powerful, that if they three alone
should

should combine, they would hold him tack; each of them being able, in a very short time to raise and bring into the Field Twenty five thousand Horse, better Troops than the *Mogols*. These Caveliers are called *Ragipouts*, or the Children of *Rajas*. They are men, who, as I have elsewhere said, carry Swords from Father to Son, and to whom the *Rajas* allot Land, on condition to be always ready to appear on Horseback, when the *Raja* commands. They can endure much hardship, and they want nothing to make them good Souldiers, but good Order and Discipline.

The *third* thing to be noted is, that the *Mogol* is a *Mahumetan*, not of the Sect called *Chias*, who follow *Aly* and his off-spring, (such as the *Persians* are, and consequently the greatest part of his Court;) but of that, which follows *Osman*, and thence are called *Osmanlys*, such as the *Turks* are. Besides, that he is a stranger, being of the Race of *Tamerlan*, who was the head of those *Mogols*, that

of the MOGOL.

that about the year 1401, over-ran *India*, where they made themselves Masters: so that he is in a Country, almost all hostile; and that the more, because not only for one *Mogol*, but in general, for one *Mahumetan*, there are hundreds of *Gentiles* or *Heathen*; which obligeth him, constantly to entertain (for his defence among so many Domestick and Potent Enemies, and against the *Persians* and *Usbecks*, his Neighbours) very great Armies, whether in time of Peace or War, as well about his Person as in the Field; as well of the People of the Countrey, (*Rajas* and *Patans*,) as chiefly *Mogolians*, or at least esteemed such because they are White, and *Mahumetans*; which sufficeth at present; his Court being no more now as 'twas at first, consisting altogether of true *Mogols*; but a mixture of all sorts of strangers, *Usbecks*, *Persians*, *Arabians*, and *Turks*, or their Children; but with this distinction, that the Children of the third or fourth generation, and that have taken the Brown colour,

and

and the soft humour of the Countrey, are not so much esteem'd as the new comers; being also seldom raised to publick Offices; but counting themselves happy, if they may serve as simple Horsemen or Foot.

Of these Armies I am now going to give you some description, that thereby knowing the great expences, which the Grand *Mogol* is obliged to be at, you may the better judge of his true Riches; let us first take a view of the Field Militia, he is necessitated to maintain.

The chief thereof are the *Rajas*, such as *Jesseignæ*, *Jessomseignæ*, and many others, to whom he allows very great pensions to have them always ready with a certain number of *Ragipouts*, esteeming them like *Omrahs*, that is, like other Strangers, and *Mahumetan* Lords; both in the Army, that is always about his person, and in those also, that are in the Field. These *Rajas* are generally obliged to the same things, that the *Omrahs* are, even to the point of keeping guard;

yet

of the MOGOL. 141

yet with this distinction, that they keep not the guard within the Fortress, as those, but without, under their Tents; they not liking to be shut up twenty four hours in a Fortress, nor so much as ever to go thither but well attended with Men resolute to be cut in pieces for their service; as hath appeared, when they have been ill dealt withal.

The *Mogol* is obliged to keep these *Rajas* in his service for sundry reasons. The *first*, because the Militia of the *Rajas* is very good (as was said above,) and because there are *Rajas*, (as was intimated also) one of whom can bring into the Field above 25000 men. The *Second*, the better to bridle the other *Rajas*, and to reduce them to reason, when they cantonize, or when they refuse to pay tribute, or when out of fear or other cause they will not go out of their Country to the Army, when the *Mogol* requireth it. The *third*, the better to nourish jealousies and keenness amongst them, by Favouring and Caressing the one more

more than the other, which is done to that degree, that they proceed to fight with one another very frequently.

The *fourth*, to employ them against the *Patans*, or against his own *Omrahs* and Governours, in case any of them should rise.

The *fifth*; to employ them against the King of *Golkonda*, when he refuseth to pay his tribute, or when he will defend the King of *Visapour*, or some *Rajas* his neighbours, which the *Mogol* hath a mind to rifle, or to make his tributaries; the *Mogol* in the those cases not daring to trust his *Omrahs* overmuch, who most are *Persians*, and not of the same Religion with him, but *Chias*, like the Kings of *Persia* and *Golkonda*.

The *sixth*, and the most considerable of all, is, to employ them against the *Persians* upon occasion; not daring then also to confide in his *Omrahs*, who for the greatest part, as was just now said, are *Persians*, and consequently have no stomach to Fight against their natural King; and the less, because

of the MOGOL.

cause they believe him to be their *Imam*, their *Caliph* or high Priest, descended from *Aly*, and against whom therefore they believe they cannot make War without a crime or a great sin.

The *Mogol* is farther obliged to entertain some *Patans* for the same, or somewhat like reasons, that he doth the *Rajas*.

At last he must entertain that stranger Militia of the *Mogols*, that we have taken notice of: And as this is the main strength of his State, and which obliges him to incredible charges, me thinks it will not be amiss to describe to you, of what nature it is, though I should be somewhat long in doing it.

Let us therefore consider, if you please, this stranger Militia, both Cavalry and Infantry, as divided into two; the *one* being always near the *Mogol's* Person; the *other*, dispersed up and down in the several Provinces. And in the Cavalry that is about his Person, let us first take notice of the *Omrahs*; then,

then, of the *Manfebdars*; next, of the *Roufindars*; laft of all, of the fimple Horfemen. From thence let us proceed to the Infantry, in which we fhall confider the Mufquetiers, and all thofe men on foot that attend the Ordnance; where fomething will occur to be faid of their Artillery.

It is not to be thought, that the *Omrahs* or Lords of the *Mogol's* Court are Sons of great Families, as in *France*; All the Lands of that Empire being the *Mogol's* propriety, it follows, that there are neither Dutchies, nor Marquifats, nor any Family Rich in Land, and fubfifting of its own income and patrimony. And often enough they are not fo much as *Omrahs* Sons, becaufe the King being Heir of all their Eftates, it is confequent that the Houfes cannot fubfift long in their greatnefs; on the contrary, they often fall and that on a fudden, infomuch that the Sons, or at leaft the Grandfons of a Potent *Omrah*, are frequently, after the death of their Father, reduced in a manner to Beggery, and

ob-

obliged to lift themselves under some *Omrah* for simple Horsemen. 'Tis true, that ordinarily the *Mogol* leaves some small pension to the Widow, and often also to the Children; or, if the Father liveth too long, he may by particular favour advance them sooner, especially if they be proper men, white of Face, having as yet not too much of the *Indian* Complexion and temper, and so passing yet for true *Mogols*: Though this advancement by favour do always proceed in a slow pace; it being almost a general custom, that a man must pass from small Pays and small Places to great ones. These *Omrahs* then are commonly but Adventurers and Strangers of all sorts of Nations, such as I have said; which draw one another to this Court; men of a mean descent, some of them slaves; most of them without instruction, which the *Mogol* thus raiseth to dignities as he thinks good, and degrades them again, as he pleaseth.

Amongst these *Omrahs*, some are *Hazary*, others *Dou Hazary*, others

Penge, Hecht, and *Deh Hazary*, and even (such as was the the Kings eldest Son) *Dovazdeh Hazary*, that is to say, Lord of a thousand Horse, of two thousand, five thousand, seven, ten, and twelve thousand; their pay being less or more in proportion to the number of Horses; I say, of Horses, because they are not paid in respect of the Horsemen, but of the Horse; the *Omrahs* having power to entertain Horsemen of two Horses a man, to be the better able to serve in the hot Countrys, where 'tis a common saying, that the Horseman that hath but one Horse, is more than half a Footman. Yet we must not think, that they are obliged to entertain, or that the King effectively pays so many Horse, as these great names of *Dovazdeh* or *Hecht Hazary* do impart, that is, 12000 or 8000 Horse. These are specious Names, to amuse and attract Strangers; the King determines the number of Horses in actual service, which they are bound to entertain, pays them according to this number; and besides that,

of the MOGOL.

that, he payes them a certain number which they are not bound to entertain; and this is that which ordinarily makes the principal part of their penſions; not to ſpeak of what they finger out of the pay of every Horſeman, and of the number of the Horſes; which certainly amounts to very conſiderable Penſions; eſpecially if they can obtain good *Jah-ghirs*, that is, good Lands for their Penſion. For I ſaw, that the Lord, under whom I was, that was a *Penge-hazary*, or one of five thouſand Horſe, and who was only obliged to entertain five hundred in effect, had, after all his Cavalry was paid, remaining for his Penſion near five thouſand Crowns a Month; though he was *Nagdy*, that is, paid in Money drawn out of the Treaſury, as all thoſe are, that have not Lands. Yet notwithſtanding all theſe great Penſions, I ſee none but very few that are rich, but many that are uneaſie and indebted: Not that they are ruined by keeping too plentiful Tables, as elſewhere great Lords frequently are;
but

but that which exhaufteth them, are the great Prefents which they are obliged to make to the King at certain Feftivals of the year, every one after the rate of his pay; next, the vaft expences they mnft be at for entertaining their Wives, Servants, Camels, and many Horfes of great value, which they keep in their particular Stables.

The number of the *Omrahs*, as well of thofe, that are in the Field in the Provinces and Armies, as of thofe that are at the Court, is very great. I never could precifely learn it; nor is it determined: But I have never feen lefs of them at Court, than twenty five or thirty, that are thus Penfionaries according to a greater or leffer number of Horfes to be entertain'd by them from 12000 downward to 1000. Thefe are the *Omrahs*, that arrive to the Governments and principal Offices of the Court and Armies; that are, as they fpeak, the Pillars of the Empire, and that keep up the fplendor of the Court never going abroad, but richly deck'd

fome

sometimes riding on Elephants, sometimes on Horseback, sometimes carried in a *Paleky* or Chair, commonly attended by a good number of Horsemen, to wit, of those that have the guard at that time, as also by many Foot-men, marching before and on his sides, to make way, to drive away the Flies, to take off the dust with Peacocks-tails, to carry water for drink, and sometimes Books of Accounts, or other Papers.

All those that are at Court, are obliged, under a considerable penalty, to come twice every day to salute the King in the Assembly, once about ten or eleven a Clock in the morning, when he renders Justice; and the second time, about six hours at night. They are also obliged by turns to keep the guard in the Castle once a week, during twenty four hours. Thither they carry at that time their Beds, Tapisseries and other Moveables, the King furnishing them with nothing but provisions of Meat and Drink, which they receive with great reverence.

rence, making a treble obeisance, with their face turned to his Apartment, their hands down to the ground, and then lifted up upon their heads. Besides, they are obliged on horseback to follow the King whithersoever he marcheth in any weather, rainy or dusty, whether he be carried in his Chair, or on an Elephant, or a Field-Throne, which last is done by eight men carrying him on their shoulders, eight others marching on his side, to relieve the others; himself being in all Marches well cover'd from the inconveniencies of the weather, whether he go to war, or to hunt, or to exercise his Souldiery. And this attendance those *Omrahs* are to give, except some of them be exempted by the *Mogol* because of their peculiar Offices, or upon the account of sickness or old age, or to avoid embarasment, as commonly 'tis practised, when he goeth only to some neighbouring Town to hunt, or to some house of pleasure, or to the Mosquee, there being then seldom any about him but those that keep the Guard that day.

Man-

of the MOGOL. 151

Manfebdars are Cavaliers of *Manfeb*, which is particular and honourable pay; not fo great indeed as that of the *Omrahs*, but much greater than that of the others; they being efteemed as little *Omrahs*, and of the rank of thofe, that are raifed to that dignity.

Thefe acknowledge alfo none for their Head but the King, and they are generally obliged to whatever we have faid the *Omrahs* are. In a word, they would be true *Omrahs*, if they had, as divers heretofore have had, fome Horfemen under them; whereas they have ordinarily but two, four, or fix Horfes having the Kings mark, and their pay goes no higher than from 400, to 600 or 700 *Roupies* a Month. Their number alfo is not fixed, but much exceeds that of the *Omrahs*, there being of them at the Court always two or three hundred, befides thofe that are in the Provinces and Armies.

Rouzindars are alfo a fort of Cavaliers, but fuch as have their pay by the day, (as the word it felf imports) which

which yet sometimes is greater than that of many *Mansebdars*, but not so honourable; but then they are not bound as the *Mansebdars*, to take at a set price (which someties is not too reasonable) of those Tapisseries and other Household-stuff, that hath served for the Kings Pallace. Their number is very great; they enter into the meane Offices, many of them being Clerks under-Clerks, Signet-men, and the like.

Simple Cavaliers, are those, that are under the *Omrahs*; amongst whom the most considerable and having most Pay are those, that have two Horses marked on the Leg with the mark of their *Omrah*. Their Pay is not absolutely fixed, but depends chiefly from the generosity of the *Omrah*, who may favour whom he pleaseth. Yet the *Mogol*'s intention is, that the Pay of a simple Cavalier or Horseman be no less than twenty five *Roupies* or thereabout a Month, stating his account with the *Omrahs* upon that Foot.

Th

of the MOGOL.

The pay of the Foot is the leaſt, and their Muſquetiers are pitiful men, unleſs they diſcharge when their Musket leans on that ſmall woodden fork hanging to it; yet even then they are afraid of ſingeing their great Beards, and of burning their Eyes, but moſt of all, leaſt ſome *Dgen* or evil ſpirit burſt their Musket. Some of theſe have 20 *Roupies* a Month, ſome 15, ſome 10. But yet there are ſome Gunners, that have great Pay, eſpecially thoſe of the *Franguis* or *Chriſtians*, as *Portugueſes*, *Engliſh*, *Dutch*, *Germans*, *French*, that retire thither from *Goa*, flying from *Engliſh* and *Dutch* Companies. Heretofore when the *Mogols* did not yet know how to manage Artillery, their Pay was very great. And there are yet ſome of that time, who have 200 *Roupies* a Month; but now they will recieve none for more than thirty two.

Their Artillery is of two ſorts; the one is the great and heavy Artillery; the other the light. As for the former,

mer, I remember, that when the King after his Sickneſs went with hi whole Army abroad into the Country diverting himſelf every day in Hunting, ſometimes of Cranes, ſometimes of the gray Oxen (a kind c Elks) ſometimes of Gazels, Leopards and Lions, and making his pro greſs towards *Lahor* and *Kachemir* (that little paradiſe of *India*) ther to paſs the Summer, the Army ha ſeventy pieces of Cannon, moſt c them caſt, not counting the two c three hundred Camels, carrying eac a ſmall Field-piece of the bigneſs of good double Muſket, faſtned to tho Animals. The other light Artiller is very brave and well order'd, con ſting of fifty or ſixty ſmall Field-piec all of Braſs, each mounted on a litt Chariot, very fine and well painte with a ſmall Coffer before and behin for the Powder, drawn by two ve fair Horſes, driven by a Coachm like a *Caleche*, adorned with a numb of ſmall red Streamers, each havi a third Horſe, led by the Chariot f relief. T

of the MOGOL.

The great Artillery could not alwayes follow the King, who often left the High-way, and turn'd sometimes to the right, sometimes to the left hand, crossing the fields, to find the true places for Game, and to follow the course of the Rivers. That therefore was to keep the High way to go the more easily, and to avoid the embarasments, which it would have met with in the ill passages, especially in those Boat-bridges made to pass Rivers. The light Artillery is inseparable from the person of the King, it marcheth away in the morning, when the King comes out of his Tent, and whereas he commonly goes a little aside into the places for Game, this Artillery passeth on straight with all possible speed, to be in time at the Rendez-vous, and there to appear before the Kings Tent, which is there made ready the day before; as are also the Tents of the great *Omrahs*: and this whole Artillery giveth a volly just when the King enters into his Tent, thereby to give notice to the Army of his arrival.

Z   The

men, and Foot and Artillery wherever any War is made. The difference is only in the number, which is much greater in the Field-Army, than in the other. For that Army alone, which the *Mogol* is conſtrained perpetually to maintain in *Decan*, to bridle the potent King of *Golkonda*, and to make War upon the King of *Viſapour*, and upon all the *Raja's* that joyn with him, muſt conſiſt at leaſt of twenty or twenty five thouſand Horſe, ſometimes of thirty.

The Kingdom of *Kaboul*, for its ordinary Guard againſt the *Perſians*, *Augans*, *Balouches*, and I know not how many Mounteniers, requireth at leaſt fifteen thouſand. The Kingdom of *Kachmire*, more than four thouſand; and the Kingdom of *Bengale*, much more; not counting thoſe that are employed in the War, which muſt almoſt alwayes be maintained on that ſide;

side; nor those which the Governors of the several Provinces do need for their defence, according to the particular extent and situation of their Governments; which maketh an incredible number.

Not to mention the Infantry (which is inconsiderable) I am apt to believe with many others, well informed of these matters, that the number of the Horse in actual service about the Kings person, comprehending the Cavalry of the *Raja's* and *Patans*, mounteth to thirty five or forty thousand; and that this number, joyned to those that is abroad in the Field, may make two hundred thousand, and better.

· I say, that the Infantry is inconsiderable; for I can hardly believe, that in the Army which is about the King, comprising the Musquetiers, and all the Gunners and their Mates, and whatever serves in this Artillery, can amount to much more than fifteen thousand; whence you may make a near guess, what the number of the Foot must be in the Field. So that

that I know not whence to take that prodigious number of Foot, which some do reckon in the Armies of the Great *Mogol*, unless it be, that with this true Souldiery they confound all the Serving-men and Victualers, that follow the Army; for in that sence I should easily believe, that they had reason to reckon two or three hundred thousand men in that Army alone which is with the King, and sometimes more; especially when 'tis certain, that he is to be long absent from the Capital City: which will not seem so strange to him, that considers the multitude and confusion of Tents, Kitchens, Baggage, Women, Elephants, Camels, Oxen, Horses, Waiting-men, Porters, Forragers, Victualers, Merchants of all sorts, that must follow the Army; nor to him, that knows the State and particular Government of that Countrey, wherein the King is the sole proprietor of all the Lands of the Kingdom; whence it necessarily follows, that a whole Metropolitan City, such as *Dehly ly* and *Agra*, liveth of almoſt nothing but of the Souldiery, and is conſequently obliged to follow the King when he taketh the Field; thoſe Towns being nothing leſs than *Paris*, but indeed no otherwiſe governed than a Camp of Armies a little better and more conveniently lodged than in the open Field.

Beſides all theſe things, you may alſo conſider, if you pleaſe, that generally all this Militia, which I have been repreſenting to you, from the greateſt *Omrah*, to the meaneſt Souldier, is indiſpenſably paid every two months; the Kings pay being its ſole refuge and relief; nor can its pay be deferred there, as 'tis ſometimes with us; where, when there are preſſing occaſions of the State, a Gentleman, an Officer, and even a ſimple Cavalier, can ſtay a while, and maintain himſelf of his own Stock, Rents and the Incomes of his Land. But in the *Mogol*'s Countrey, all muſt be paid at the time prefix'd, or all disbands and ſtarves, after they have ſold that little they have; as I ſaw in this laſt War,

that

that many were going to do, if it had not soon ceased. And this the more, because that in all this Militia there is almost no Souldier that hath not wife and children, servants and slaves, that look for this pay, and have no other hope of relief. And hence it is, that many wonder, considering the huge number of persons living of pay (which amounts to millions) whence such vast Revenues can be had for such excessive Charges: Although this need not to be so much wondred at, considering the Riches of the Empire, the peculiar Government of the State, and the said universal propriety of the Sovereign.

You may add to all this, that the Grand *Mogol* keeps nigh him at *Dehly* and *Agra*, and thereabout, two or three thousand brave Horses, to be always ready upon occasion; as also eight or nine hundred Elephants, and a vast number of Mules, Horses, and Porters, to carry all the great Tents and their Cabinets, to carry his Wives, Kitchens, Houshold-stuff,

Ganges-

of the MOGOL.

Ganges-Water, and all the other Neceffaries for the Field, which he hath always about him as if he were at home; things not abfolutely neceffary in our Kingdoms.

To this may be added thofe incredible Expences upon the *Seraglio*, more indifpenfable than will be eafily believed; that vaft ftore of fine Linnen, Cloth of Gold, Embroideries, Silks, Musk, Amber, Pearls, fweet Effences, &c. confumed there.

All thefe Charges being put together, and compared with the Revenues the *Mogol* may be thought to have, it will be eafie to judge, whether he be indeed fo very rich as he is made to be. As for me, I very well know, that it cannot be denied, that he hath very great Revenues; I believe, he hath more alone than the *Grand Seignior* and the King of *Perfia* both together: But then, to believe all thofe extravagant Stories made of the vaftnefs of his Revenues, is a thing I could never do: And if I fhould believe the beft part

a small Knife, which was all the Arms that were left him. One of these Butchers immediately fell upon *Sepe-Chekouh*; the others, upon the arms and legs of *Dara*, throwing him to the ground, and holding him under, 'till *Nazer* cut his throat. His Head was forthwith carried to the Fortress to *Aureng-Zebe*, who presently commanded it to be put in a dish, and that water should be fetch'd; which when brought, he wiped it off with an Handkerchief, and after he had caused the Face to be washed clean, and the blood done away, and was fully satisfied that it was the very head of *Dara*, he fell a weeping, and said these words; Ah *Bed-bakt*! Ah unfortunate Man! Take it away, and bury it in the Sepulchre of *Houmayon*.

At night, the Daughter of *Dara* was brought into the *Seraglio*, but afterwards sent to *Chah-Jehan*, and *Begum-Saheb*, who asked her of *Aureng-Zebe*. Concerning *Dara*'s Wife, she had ended her days before at *Lahor*: She had poyson'd her self, foreseeing the

the extremities she was falling into, together with her Husband. *Sepe-Chekouh* was sent to *Goualeor*. And after a few days, *Gion-kan* was sent for, to come before *Aureng-Zebe* in the Assembly: To him were given some Presents, and so he was sent away; but being near his Lands, he was rewarded according to his desert, being killed in a Wood. This barbarous Man not knowing, or not considering, that if Kings do sometimes permit such Actions for their Interest, yet they abhor them, and sooner or later revenge them.

In the mean time, the Governour of *Tatabakar*, by the same Orders that had been required of *Dara*, was obliged to surrender the Fortress. It was indeed upon such a composition as he would have, but it was also with an intention not to keep word with him. For the poor Eunuch, arriving at *Lahor*, was cut in pieces, together with those few Men he had then with him, by *Kalil-ullah-kan*, who was Governour thereof. But the reason of the

The *other* is, That all this Treasure of *Chah-jehan*, who was very frugal, and had Reigned above forty Years without considerable Wars, never mounted to six *Kourours* of *Roupies*. A *Roupy* is about twenty nine pence. An hundred thousand of them make a *Lecque*, and an hundred *Lecques* make one *Kourour*. *'Tis true, I do not comprehend in this great Treasure that great abundance of Gold-smiths work, so variously wrought in Gold and Silver; nor that vast store of precious Stones and Pearls of a very high value. I doubt, whether there be any King in the World that hath more. The Throne alone, cover'd with them, is valued at least three *Kourours*, if I remember aright; But then, it is to be consider'd also, that they are the spoils of those ancient Princes, the *Patans* and *Rajas*, gathered and piled up from Immemorial times, and still increasing from one King to another, by the Presents which the

* So that the six Kourours would make about seven Millions and an half English Money.

he *Omrahs* are obliged yearly at cer-
ain Feſtival-days to make him; and
vhich are eſteemed to be the Jewels
f the Crown, which it would be
riminal to touch, and upon which
King of *Mogol* in caſe of neceſſity
vould find it very hard to procure the
:aſt Sum.

But before I conclude, I ſhall take
otice, whence it may proceed, that
hough this Empire of *Mogol* be thus
n Abyſs of Gold and Silver, (as hath
een ſaid,) yet notwithſtanding there
ppears no more of it among the Peo-
le, than elſewhere; yea, rather that
he People is there leſs Monied than
1 other places.

The *firſt* reaſon is, that much of it
; conſumed in melting over and over
ll thoſe Noſe and Ear-rings, Chains,
'inger-rings, Bracelets of Hands
nd Feet, which the Women wear,
ut chiefly in that incredible quantity
f Manufactures, wherein ſo much
; ſpent, which is loſt, as in all thoſe
imbroideries, Silk-ſtuffs, enter-
voven with Gold and Silver, Cloath,
Scarfs,

Scarf, Turbants, &c. of the same: For generally all that Militia loveth to be guided from the *Omrahs* to the meanest Souldiers with their Wives and Children, though they should starve at home.

The *second*, That all the Lands of the Kingdom being the Kings propriety, they are given either as Benefices, which they call *Jah-ghirs*, or, as in *Turky*, *Timars*, to men of the Militia for their Pay or Pension (as the word *Jah-ghir* imports:) Or else they are given to the Governours for their Pension, and the entertainment of their Troops, on condition that of the surplus of those Land-revenues they give yearly a certain sum to the King, as Farmers; Or, lastly, the King reserveth them for himself as a particular Domaine of his House, which never or very seldom are given as *Jah-ghirs*, and upon which he keeps Farmers, who also must give him a yearly sum; which is to say, that the *Timariots*, *Governours* and *Farmers* have an absolute Authority over the Country-

of the MOGOL.

y-men, and even a very great one
er the Tradef-men and Merchants
the Towns, Boroughs, and Vil-
ges, depending from them: fo that
thofe parts there are neither great
ords nor Parliaments, nor Prefidial
ourts, as amongft us, to keep thefe
eople in awe; nor *Kadis* or Judges
owerful enough to hinder and reprefs
eir violence; Nor, in a word, any
erfon, to whom a Country-man,
radef-man, or Merchant, can make
s complaints to, in cafes of extor-
on and tyranny, often practifed up-
1 them, by the Souldiery and Go-
ernours, who every where do im-
nely abufe the Authority Royal,
hich they have in hand, unlefs it be
erhaps a little in thofe places that are
ear to Capital Cities, as *Dehly* and
gra, and in great Towns, and con-
derable Sea-ports of the Provinces,
hence they know that the com-
laints can be more eafily conveyed to
he Court. Whence it is, that all
d every one ftand in continual fear
f thefe People, efpecially of the
Gover-

Governours more than any Slave doth of his Master: that ordinarily they affect to appear poor and Money-less very mean in their Apparel, Lodging Houshold-stuff, and yet more in Meat and Drink; that often they apprehend even to meddle with Trade, lest they should be thought Rich, and so fall into the danger of being ruined. So that at last they find no other remedy to secure their Wealth, than to hide and dig their Money deep under Ground, thus getting out of the ordinary commerce of Men, and so Dying, neither the King nor the State having any benefit by it. Which is a thing not only happens among the Peasants and Artizans, but (which is far more considerable) amongst all sorts of Merchants, whether *Mahumetans* or *Heathens*, except some that are in the Kings, or some *Omrahs* Pay, or that have some particular Patron and support in power: But principally among the *Heathen*, which are almost the only Masters of the Trade and Money, infatuated with the belief,

lief, that the Gold and Silver, which they hide in their life-time, shall serve them after death. And this, in my opinion, is the true reason, why there appears so little Money in Trade among the People.

But thence ariseth a Question very considerable, *viz.* Whether it were not more expedient, not only for the Subjects, but for the State it self, and for the Sovereign, not to have the Prince such a Proprietor of the Lands of the Kingdom, as to take away the *Meum* and *Tuum* amongst private persons; as 'tis with us? For my part, after a strict comparing the State of our Kingdoms, where that *Meum* and *Tuum* holds, with that of those other Kingdoms, where it is not, I am thoroughly perswaded, that it is much better and more beneficial for the Sovereign himself, to have it so as 'tis in our parts. Because that in those parts where 'tis otherwise, the Gold and Silver is lost, as I was just now observing: There is almost no person secure from the violences of those

those Timariots, Governours, and Farmers: The Kings, how well soever they be disposed toward their people, are never almost in a condition (as I lately noted) to get Justice administred to them, and to hinder tyrannies; especially in those great Dominions, and in the Provinces remote from the Capital Towns; Which yet ought to be, as doubtless it is, one of the chief employments and considerarations of a King. Besides, this tyranny often grows to that excess, that it takes away what is necessary to the life of a Peasant or Tradesman, who is starved for hunger and misery, who gets no Children, or if he does, sees them die young for want of food; or that abandons his Land, and turns some Cavalier's man, or flies whither he may to his neighbours, in hopes of finding a better condition. In a word, the Land is not tilled but almost by force, and consequently very ill, and much of it is quite spoiled and ruined, there being none to be found, that can or will be at the charge of entertaining the

ditches

ditches and channels for the courſe of waters to be conveyed to neceſſary places ; nor any body that care to build Houſes, or to repair thoſe that are ruinous; the Peaſant reaſoning thus with himſelf: Why ſhould I toil ſo much for a Tyrant that may come to morrow to take all away from me, or at leaſt all the beſt of what I have, and not leave, if the fancy taketh him, ſo much as to ſuſtain my life even very poorly ? And the Timariot, the Governour and the Farmer, will reaſon thus with himſelf ; Why ſhould I beſtow Money and take pains of bettering or maintaining this Land, ſince I muſt every hour expect to have it taken from me, or exchanged for another ? I labour neither for my ſelf nor for my Children ; and that place which I have this year, I may perhaps have no more the next. Let us draw from it what we can, whilſt we poſſeſs it, though the Peaſant ſhould break or ſtarve, though the Land ſhould become a deſert, when I am gone!

And for this very reaſon it is, that we
A a ſee

see those vast Estates in *Asia* go so wretchedly and palpably to ruin. Thence it is, that throughout those parts we see almost no other Towns but made up of earth and dirt; nothing but ruin'd and deserted. Towns and Villages, or such as are going to ruin. Even thence it is, that we see (for Example) those *Mesopotamia's*, *Anatolia's*, *Palestina's*, those admirable plains of *Antioch*, and so many other Lands, anciently so well tilled, so fertile, and so well peopled, at the present half deserted, untill'd, and bandon'd, or become pestilent and uninhabitable bogs. Thence it is also, that of those incomparable Lands of *Egypt* it is observed, that within less than *four-score* years, more than the *tenth* part of it is lost, no people being to be found, that will expend what is necessary to maintain all the Channels, and to restrain the River *Nile* from violently overflowing on one hand, and so drowning too much the low Lands, or from covering them with Sand, which cannot be removed from thence but
with

of the MOGOL.

with great pains and charges. From the same root it comes, that Arts are languishing in those Countries, or at least flourish much less than else they would do, or do with Us. For what heart and spirit can an Artizan have to study well, and to apply his mind to his work, when he sees, that among the people, which is for the most part beggerly or will appear so, there is none that considers the goodness and neatness of his Work, every body looking for what is cheap? and that the Grandees pay them but very ill and when they please? The poor Tradesmen often thinking himself happy, that he can get clear from them without the *Korrah*, which is that terrible whip, that hangs nigh the gate of the *Omrahs*: Further, when he seeth that there is no help at all ever to come to any thing, as to buy an Office, or some Land for himself and Children, and that even he dares not appear to have a peny in cash, or to wear good cloaths, or to eat a good meal, for fear he should be thought rich. And indeed the beauty and exactness of Arts had been quite lost in those parts long ago, if it were not that the Kings and Grandees there did give wages to certain Workmen, that work in their Houses, and there teach their Children, and endeavour to make themselves able in order to be a little more considered, and to escape the *Korrah*; and if also it were not, that those great and rich Merchants of Towns, who are protected by good and powerful Patrons, pay'd those workmen a little better: I say, *a little Better*; for, what fine stuffs soever we see come from those Countreys, we must not imagine, that the workman is there in any honour, or comes to any thing; 'tis nothing but meer necessity or the cudgel, that makes him work, he never grows rich; it is no small matter, when he hath wherewith to live and to cloath himself narrowly. If their be any Money to gain of the work, that is not for him, but for those great Merchants of Towns, I was just now speaking of; and even these themselves find it often difficult enough

nough to maintain themselves, and to prevent extorsion.

'Tis from the same cause also, that a gross and profound ignorance reigns in those States. For how is it possible, there should be Academies and Colleges well founded, where are such Founders to be met with? And if there were any, whence were the Schollars to be had? Where are those that have means sufficient to maintain their Children in Colleges? And if there were, who would appear to be so rich? And if they would, where are those Benefices, Preferments and Dignities that require knowledge and abilities, and that may animate young men to study?

Thence it is likewise, that Traffick languishes in all that Country, in comparison of ours. For how many are there, that care to take pains, to run up and down, to write much, and to run danger for another, for a Governour, that shall extort, if he be not in league with some considerable sword-man, whose slave he in a manner is, and that

that makes his own cond
him?

It is not there, that the
for their service, Princes, L
tlemen, sons of rich and
lies, Officers, Citizens, Me
even Tradef-men well-borr
cated, and well-inftructe
courage, that have a true a
refpect for their King, tha
a great while at the Court
Army at their own expen
taining themfelves with g
and content with the fav
pect of the Prince; and
occafion fight manfully,
uphold the honour of their
and Families. Thofe Kings,
fee about them but men o
Slaves, Ignorants, Brutes
Courtizans as are raifed fro
to dignities, and that for wa
education and inftruction
ways retain fomewhat of
fpring, of the temper of be
riched, proud, unfufferable
infenfible of honour, dif-i

and void of affection and regard for the honour of their King & Countrey. Here it is, where thofe Kings muft ruine all, to find means to defray all thofe prodigious Charges, which they cannot avoid for entertaining their great Court, which hath no other fource to fubfift but their Coffers and Treafure, and for maintaining conftantly the vaft number of Souldiers, neceffary for them to keep the People in fubjection, to prevent their running away, to make them work, and to get what is exacted from them, they being fo many Defperado's, for being perpetually under hatches, and for labouring only for others.

Thence it is alfo, that in an important War that may happen (which may be almoft at all times) they muft almoft of neceffity fell the Government for ready Money and immenfe Sums; whence chiefly that ruine and defolation comes to pafs which we fee. For the Governour, which is the Buyer, muft not he be re-imburfed of all thofe great Sums of Money, which he hath

A a 4   taken

taken up, perhaps the third or fourth part, at high interest? Must not a Governour also, whether he have bought the Government or not, find means as well as a Timariot and a Farmer, to make every year great Presents to a *Visir*, an *Eunuch*, a Lady of the *Seraglio*, and to those other persons, that support him at Court? Must he not pay to the King his usual Tributes, and withal enrich himself, that wretched Slave, half famish'd and deeply indebted when he first appeared, without Goods, Lands, and revenues of his House; such as they all are? Do not they ruin all, and lay all waste; I mean those, that in the Provinces are like so many small Tyrants with a boundless and unmeasured Authority, there being no body there, as hath been already said, that can restrain them, or to whom a Subject can have refuge, to save himself from their tyranny and to obtain justice?

'Tis true, that in the Empire of the *Mogol* the *Vakea-nevis*, that is, those Persons, whom he sends into the Provinces

vinces to write to him whatever paſſeth there, do a little keep the Officers in awe, provided they do not collude together (as it almoſt always happens) to devour all; as alſo that the Governments are not there ſo often ſold, nor ſo openly as in *Turky* ; I ſay, *not ſo openly* (for thoſe great Preſents, they are from time to time obliged to make, are almoſt equivalent to Sales) and that the Governors ordinarily remain longer in their Governments; which maketh them not ſo hungry, ſo beggarly, and ſo deep in debt, as thoſe new Comers, and that conſequently they do not always tyrannize over the people with ſo much cruelty ; even apprehending, leſt they ſhould run away to the *Raja's* ; which yet falls out very often.

'Tis alſo true, that in *Perſia* the Governments are not ſo frequently nor ſo publickly ſold as in *Turky* ; the Sons of the Governors alſo ſucceding often enough to their Fathers ; which is alſo the cauſe, that the people there is often not ſo ill treated as in *Turky*, and

occa-

occasions withal, that there is more politeness, and that even some there are that addict themselves to study. But all that is really but a slight matter; those three States of *Turky*, *Persia* and *Indostan*, forasmuch as they have all three taken away the *Meum* and *Tuum* as to Land and Propriety of possessions (which is the foundation of whatever is good and regular in the world) cannot but very near resemble one another: they have the same defect, they must at last, sooner or later, needs fall into the same inconveniencies, which are the necessary consequences of it, *viz*, Tyranny, Ruine, and Desolation.

Far be it therefore, that our Monarchs of *Europe* should thus be proprietors of all the Lands which their Subjects possess. Their Kingdoms would be very far from being so well cultivated and peopled, so well built, so rich, so polite and flourishing as we see them. Our Kings are otherwise rich and powerful; and we must avow that we are much better and more royally ferved. There would be Kings of Defarts and Solitudes, of Beggars and Barbarians, fuch as thofe are whom I have been reprefenting ; who, becaufe they will have all, at laft lofe all ; and who, becaufe they will make themfelves too rich, at length find themfelves without riches, or, at leaft, very far from that which they covet after, out of their blind ambition and paffion of being more abfolute than the Laws of God and Nature do permit. For, where would be thofe Princes, thofe Prelates, thofe Nobles, thofe rich Citizens and great Merchants, and thofe famous Artizans, thofe Towns of *Paris*, *Lyons*, *Thoulouse*, *Rouën*, *London*, and fo many others? Where would be that infinite number of Burroughs and Villages, all thofe fair Countreyhoufes, and Fields, and Hillocks tilled and maintained with fo much induftry, care and labour? And where would confequently be all thofe vaft Revenues drawn thence, which at laft enrich the Subjects and the Sovereign both? We fhould find the great Cities,

ties, and the great Burroughs rendred inhabitable becaufe of the ill Air, and to fall to ruine without any bodies taking care of repairing them; the hillocks abandoned, and the fields overfpred with the bufhes, or filled with Peftilential Marifhes, as hath been already intimated.

A word to our dear and experienc'd Travellers: They would not find thofe fair conveniencies of travelling; they would be obliged to carry all things with them, like the *Bohemians*; and all thofe good Inns, for example, that are found between *Paris* and *Lyons*, would be like ten or twelve wretched *Caravans-ferrahs*, that is, great Barns, raifed and paved, fuch as our *Pont-neuf* is, where hundreds of men are found pel-mel together with their Horfes, Mules and Camels, where one is ftifled with heat in Summer, and ftarved of cold in Winter, if it were not for the breathing of thofe Animals, that warm the place a little.

But it will be faid, we fee fome States, where the *Meum* and *Tuum* is

not

not (as for example, that of the Grand *Seignor*, which we know better than any, without going so far as the *Indies*) that do not only subsist, but are also very powerful, and encrease daily.

'Tis true, that that State of the Grand *Seignor*, of such a prodigious extent as it is, having so vast a quantity of Lands, the Soil of which is so excellent, that it cannot be destroyed but very difficultly, and in a long time, is yet rich and populous; but it is certain also, that if it were cultivated and peopled proportionably to ours (which it would be, if there were propriety among the Subjects throughout) it would be a quite different thing; it would have people enough to raise such prodigious Armies as in old times, and rich enough to maintain them. We have travelled through almost all the parts of it; we have seen how strangely it is ruin'd and unpeopled; and how in the Capital City there now need three whole Months to raise five or six thousand men. We know also, what it would have come to ere this,
if

if it had not been for the great number of Chriſtian Slaves, that are brought into it from all parts. And no doubt but that, if the ſame Government were continued there for a number of years, that State would deſtroy it ſelf, and at laſt, fall by its own weakneſs, as it ſeems that already it is hardly maintained but only by that means, I mean, by the frequent change of Governors; there being not one Governor, nor any one man in the whole Empire, that hath a penny to enable him to maintain the leaſt thing, or that can almoſt find any men, if he had Money. A ſtrange manner to make States to ſubſiſt! There would need no more for making an end of the Seditions, than a *Brama* of *Pegu*, who killed the half of the Kingdom with hunger, and turned it into Foreſts, hindring for ſome years the Lands from being tilled, though yet he hath not ſucceeded in his Deſign, and the State have afterwards been divided, and that even lately *Ava*, the Capital Town, was upon the point of being

ing taken by an handful of *China*-fugitives. Mean time we muſt confeſs, that we are not like to ſee in our dayes that total ruine and deſtruction of this Empire we are ſpeaking of (if ſo be we ſee not ſomething worſe) becauſe it hath Neighbors, that are ſo far from being able to undertake any thing againſt him, that they are not ſo much as in a condition to reſiſt him, unleſs it be by thoſe ſuccours of ſtrangers, which the remoteneſs and jealouſie would make ſlow, ſmall, and ſuſpect.

But it might be yet further objected, that it appears not, why ſuch States as theſe might not have good Laws, and why the people in the Provinces might not be enabled to come and make their complaints to a Grand *Viſir*, or to the King himſelf. 'Tis true, that they are not altogether deſtitute of good Laws, and that, if thoſe which are amongſt them were obſerved, there would be as good living there, as in any part of the world. But what are thoſe Laws good for, if they be not obſerved,

ved, and if there be no means to make them to be executed? Is it not the Grand *Vifir*, or the King that appoints for the people fuch beggarly Tyrants, and that hath no others to fet over them? Is it not He that fells thofe governments? Hath a poor Peafant or Tradefman means to make great journeys, and to come and feek for Juftice in the Capital City, remote perhaps 150 or 200 Leagues from the place of his abode? Will not the Governour caufe him to be made away in his journey (as it hath often hapned) or catch him fooner or later? And will he not provide his Friends at Court, to fupport him there, and to reprefent things quite otherwife than they are? In a word, this Governour, hungry as well as the Timariots and Farmers (that are all men for drawing Oyl out of Sand, as the *Perfian* fpeaks, and for ruining a world, with their heap of Women-harpies, Children and Slaves) this Governor, I fay, is he not the abfolute Mafter, the Super-intendant of Juftice, the Parliament, the Receiver, and all? It

that the remedy would be an hundred times worse than the Disease, considering those great inconveniences that would follow thereupon, and that in all probability the Magistrates would become such as those of the *Asiatick* States, who deserve not that Name; for in a word, our Kings have yet cause to glory upon the account of good Magistracy under them. In those parts, some Merchants excepted, Justice is only among the meanest sort of people, that are poor and of an unequal condition, who have not the means of corrupting the Judges, and to buy false Witnesses, that are there in great numbers, and very cheap, and never punished. And this I have learn'd every where by the experience of many years, and by my solicitous enquiries made among the people of the Country, and our old Merchants that are in those parts, as also of Ambassadors, Consuls and Interpreters; whatever our common Travellers may say, who, upon their having seen by chance, when they passed by, two or three

three Porters, or others of the like Gang, about a *Kady*, quickly difpatching one or other of the parties, and fometimes both, with fome lafhes under the fole of their feet, or with a *Maybalé Baba*, fome mild words, when there is no wool to fheer; who, I fay, upon fight of this, come hither, and cry out, O the good and fhort Juftice! O what honeft Judges are thofe in refpect of ours! Not confidering in the mean time, that if one of thofe wretches, that is in the wrong, had a couple of Crowns to corrupt the *Kady*, or his Clerks, and as much to buy two falfe witneffes, he might either win his procefs, or prolong it as long as he pleafed.

In conclufion, to be fhort, I fay, that the taking away this Propriety of Lands among private men, would be infallibly to intoduce at the fame time Tyranny, Slavery, Injuftice, Beggery, Barbarifm, Defolation, and to open a high way for the ruine and deftruction of Mankind, and even of Kings and States: Aud that on the contrary;
this

of the MOGOL.

this *Meum* and *Tuum*, accompanied with the hopes that every one shall keep, what he works and labours for, for himself and his Children, as his own, is the main foundation of whatever is regular and good in the World: Insomuch that whosoever shall cast his eyes upon the different Countries and Kingdoms, and taketh good notice of what follows upon this Propriety of Sovereigns, or that of the People, will soon find the true source and chief cause of that great difference we see in the several States and Empires of the world, and avow, that this is in a manner that which changes and diversifieth the Face of the whole Earth.

FINIS.

The Relation of a Voyage into *Mauritania* in *Africk*, by *Roland Frejus* of *Marseilles*, by the *French* King's Order, 1666. To *Muley Arxid*, King of *Tafiletta*, &c. For the establishment of a Commerce in the Kingdom of *Fez*, and all his other Conquests. With a Letter in Answer to divers curious Questions concerning the Religion, Manners and Customs of his Countries: Also their Trading to *Tombutum* for Gold, and divers other Particulars; by one who lived five and twenty years in the Kingdom of *Sus* and *Morocco*. Printed at *Paris*, 1670. *Englished*, 1671. 8°, Price 1 s 6 d. Sold by *M. Pitt*, at the *Angel* near the Little North-Door of St *Paul*.

Whitehall, April 24. 1679.

By Petition and Licence of the Right Honorable Sir John Trevor, His Majesties principal Secretary of State, this Continuation of the Members to Mist Benoni concerning the Empire of the Great Mogul, being rendered into English, may be printed and published.

JOHN COOKE

Whitehall, April 24. 1671.

By Permission and License of the Right Honourable Sir *John Trevor*, His Majesties principal Secretary of State, this Continuation of the *Memoires* of *Monf. Bernier*, concerning the Empire of the *Great Mogol*, being rendred into *English*, may be printed and published.

JOHN COOKE.

www.ingramcontent.com/pod-product-compliance
Lightning Source LLC
Chambersburg PA
CBHW031415230426
43668CB00007B/314